BUILD

BUILD

A BLUEPRINT FOR CONSTRUCTING **SUCCESS** IN **LEADERSHIP** AND **LIFE**

DOUG REITZ

Publishing support provided by
Ignite Press
55 Shaw Ave. Suite 204
Clovis, CA 93612
www.IgnitePress.us

ISBN: 979-8-9909287-0-1
ISBN: 979-8-9909287-1-8 (Hardcover)
ISBN: 979-8-9909287-2-5 (E-book)

For bulk purchases and for booking, contact:

Doug Reitz
build@dougreitz.blog
Beabuilder.blog

Library of Congress Control Number: 2024910236

Cover design by sala_ud_din | 99Designs
Edited by Claudia Volkman
Interior design by Jetlaunch

FIRST EDITION

This book is dedicated to my mom and dad, Lucille and Richard, my wife, Jodi, my son, Nolan, and my daughter, Molly Jane.

ACKNOWLEDGMENTS

Tim, Aya, Cole, Joe, Dawnette, Mark, and all of the designers, inspectors, consultants, clients, friends, and contractors who share the "builder" philosophy every day.

TABLE OF CONTENTS

PREFACE

You may be in a leadership role in which you are leading a team but feeling like the team is not performing. You may be on a team where you feel that nothing is ever good enough for your leader. It could be that you are a good leader and inspiring your team, but you feel like something is missing to take things to the next level.

What is holding you back from effectively leading your team, meeting your leader's goals, or taking your own leadership to another level?

At first glance, you may be inclined to say you are frustrated with the lack of communication, trust, information, direction, or understanding of the goal. Or maybe you're frustrated with the lack of drive, skill, or motivation from the people around you. You may be right. There is a gap that needs to be spanned to move forward effectively as a team.

I want you to flip your perspective 180 degrees. Instead of thinking of those frustrations as a hindrance, think of them as a starting point. They become the raw material—the bricks and mortar that form the need to find a solution. This allows you to see a problem not as an insurmountable barrier but as a bridge that needs to be built to span the gap causing the challenge, conflict, or frustration.

In every challenge or frustration, stop and ask yourself two questions:

1. What is holding me back?
2. What do I need to build to bridge the gap?

The answer is not always easy to hear. It may be *YOU* who is holding you back. You may need to change something you are doing to be more effective in the long run. You may need to help someone on your team by having a difficult conversation with them to allow them to grow and be more effective.

During the first half of my career, I was very driven to succeed and thought everything could be solved with energy and hard work. I had a mindset that I had to keep going no matter what, driving the team toward each milestone: foundations, structures, and finishes. I may have made people mad, hurt relationships, and left a path of destruction in my wake at times, but I thought the only way to be successful was to get the project done.

That, my friends, is when everything came crashing down, as you will soon learn in Chapter 1. I learned some valuable lessons during some exceedingly difficult times. I see now that it wasn't a failure but a starting point.

I learned that I needed to evolve my leadership skills beyond individual drive and success. It's not merely about personal achievement or business success; it's about the collective elevation, shared growth, and collaborative resolution of challenges and conflicts. This book hinges not just on building oneself but on the deliberate construction of others, relationships, and resolution of conflict and problems.

Limited success awaits those who fail to recognize how personal growth and the development of those around you is true success. A leader is not just a visionary but a builder—a person who constructs a foundation of trust, consensus, and shared wisdom. This blueprint for effective leadership is rooted in the principles of listening, planning, and building together. Listen. Plan. Build.

The essence of this book lies in its distinction between good leaders and great leaders. Great leaders are builders of knowledge, teams, consensus, trust, solutions, and momentum for themselves and everyone around them. Building is one of the most powerful tools a leader can have in their toolbox. The transformation from a good leader to a great leader heralds a shift in mindset—from individual success to collective advancement.

The methodology outlined here—Listen Plan Build—is more than a strategic guide. It's a philosophy, a mindset, a way of being that will propel you toward being the most effective leader possible. Listening becomes the bedrock for understanding, planning the roadmap for collective action, and building—the culmination of shared efforts to create sustainable solutions.

This book is your blueprint, guiding you through everyday conflicts and challenges and offering a framework that not only resolves immediate issues but also paves the way for enduring success. It's a call to action—to embrace the identity of a builder and wield consensus, relationships, knowledge, and momentum as tools for transformative leadership.

INTRODUCTION

You have been a builder your entire life! It's something you've learned from early childhood experiences but somehow have forgotten as you moved into a leadership position.

When you learned to walk, you did it a little bit at a time, and your parents most likely cheered when you took a few steps and fell. They cheered when you failed. Well, you can look at it that way, but they cheered because of the few steps of progress you made. After a while, you built on those few steps to be 10, 20, and 30 steps until you were walking. You have probably heard the phrase *you must walk before you can run*. That's the idea of being a builder. You build on past failures and successes to grow.

Similarly, when you learned to ride a bike, it was a process. You may have had a bike with training wheels. The training wheels kept you from falling and let you learn how to steer and pedal. Then came the day the training wheels came off; you were nervous and excited all at the same time. With you in the seat and your mom or dad behind you holding the seat, they pushed you along, holding on tight in the beginning. They let you waver back and forth so you could learn how to keep your balance. Time after time, they would run behind you, letting go a little longer each time. Every time you fell, they would encourage you to get back up and try again. Even though some of those falls were painful, you got back up, right? Eventually you were riding on your own—they were still running behind you, but you didn't know they were no longer holding on to the seat. I still remember the feeling of riding down the sidewalk in front of my house as I heard my dad yelling, "You did it! You're riding on your own!"

If you're like me and have kids, you have now come full circle because now you're the one pushing your child on a bike. The pride I felt when I let go of Nolan's and Molly's seat and yelled "You're doing it! You're riding by yourself!" was 10 times more exciting than when my dad cheered me on.

Please take a moment and remember that feeling. It's the core feeling of being a builder. When you do something for the first time or you help someone experience something new and succeed, that's just one of the many facets of what being a builder is all about.

Who Has Been a Builder in YOUR Life?

All the great leaders, mentors, managers, and friends in your life have been builders. Think about the people who have had the most impact in your life. I will guarantee that they were people who helped you through a challenge or helped you grow in skill or confidence. They were builders. As a leader, your purpose is to take a step back from any challenging situation to be able to see both sides and the middle of the challenge and then lead your team with the purpose of finding the best solution for the project. For my purpose, I want to define the word *project* as any challenge you may face. I will go deeper into this later in the book. As you can see from the stories above, and maybe from your own memories and experiences:

- Being a builder will help you counteract the desire for a quick fix or quick reward. It will help you bring people out of their corners and to the table to discuss issues. It will help you lead people to believe that it should be about the team and not the individual—that it's about the project and what's best for the cause you may be striving to attain as a team.

- Being a builder is a long-term process to support the people around you until they can "ride" on their own. It could be building a new skill, building a solution to a challenge, or building a relationship. Building is moving your team toward a cause bigger than yourself.

- Being a builder is allowing yourself to fail and learn. It's being better and doing things differently in the future to be more effective and efficient than you were in the past.

- Being a builder whenever challenges arise is the solution to getting to your goal.

- Being a builder is the quality that will make you a stronger leader as you lead your team through the challenges they face every day.

Remember, in every learning experience, challenge, or failure, there is a gap—something that needs to be done, implemented, or accomplished. Something needs to be built to span the gap.

Building Will Bridge the Gap

Another way you can look at challenges is to picture yourself on the shore of a river. The other shore has the thing you would like to do or have. The goal may be learning a new skill, developing a relationship, or solving a conflict. The river is too fast and too deep to wade or swim across. It seems impossible to reach your goal. Standing on the shore, you know where you are and can see where you want to be, but the river is the thing that stops you. You must build a bridge in order to get across it. If the gap is conflict, you need to build a bridge of consensus; if it is a relationship, you need to build a bridge of trust; and if it is a new skill, you need to build a bridge of knowledge and technique.

For example, you may disagree on the price of a certain product. Sitting across the table, you must build a solution, build consensus, or maybe build trust to reach an agreement of the price. If you are on opposite sides of the river, you need to build some kind of a bridge to get to the other side so you can walk next to the person or reach the thing you want. The people you are dealing with need to feel that you are on their side and collaborating with them.

If you are trying to build a personal relationship, you need to start with building trust or building common ground. Everything can be built if you have the right tools. In everything you do, you need to build something to allow the situation to grow and evolve.

The first bridge ever built was not the Golden Gate Bridge. Your challenge may seem as overwhelming as building a bridge over San Francisco Bay. However, the first bridge builders started small, stacking stones over small creeks and rivers, leaving a small arch for the water to pass through. They did not have the knowledge or technology to build longer spans yet. Over the years, bridge building exploded with new knowledge, science, and technology, and the spans became longer and longer.

Just like actual bridge builders, your conflict, relationship, or skill will not be built overnight. You may not have the tools, skills, or materials to get there today, but you can start developing those things so you will be able to do it in a day, a month, or a year.

The Purpose

The purpose of this book is to highlight the lessons I learned from Tim Marsh, the failures he and many others helped me through, and how we can all walk through our life being a builder. Over the last 33 years, Tim has transitioned from being my boss to being a mentor and friend, and he is someone I confide in to this day.

I will show you why you should focus on being a builder and how this can be used every day in your life. I will show you the simple steps of how to build a bridge for the gaps and challenges you are facing. No matter the challenge, whether you are building a team, building a process, building knowledge, building consensus, or building a relationship, the steps are the same.

To be a builder, you must walk alongside the people with whom you are working. Once you have established a relationship and trust, you can lead from the front, middle, or back with ease and then jump in and be a builder when needed.

The Process

This book describes the time-tested principles and concepts of how to be a builder in everything you do. You will learn the five tools of a builder I have successfully implemented at my construction company and how you can effectively use those tools to improve your projects with your own clients, design partners, and subcontractors in your community. The five tools are:

1. Know where you are and where you want to go.
2. Know how to define the real problem.
3. Learn the process of Listen Plan Build.
4. Develop the four mindsets:
    a. Solve the problem.
    b. Focus on what you can do.
    c. Always be curious.
    d. Always improve your situation.
5. Be a builder in everything you do every day.

The stories in the book will show you examples that support the concept of being a builder at work and at home, improving yourself, solving problems, and bringing people together with the techniques used in the construction industry every day.

I will give you a look into the world of construction from both a technical and cultural view. My hope is that you will see construction as an example of how to build culture, people, and processes throughout your life as well as build trust and respect for the companies and people you work with. When you look around at the people and places you meet daily, look for the good and embrace it. That's what you need to do as a builder. Do not ignore the negatives because part of being a builder is seeing problems and building solutions. A proactive, positive outlook that focuses on what we have in common and how things can change for the better is the mindset of a builder.

In construction, through all the hardship, construction workers see the long-term reward of what they are doing for the people around them—a cause bigger than themselves, if you will. That cause and the pure energy and drive of the people are what carry them through the long hours in the heat and the cold to provide structures that serve and improve our community.

If you have ever felt stuck, frustrated, or could not see a solution, this book will give you the tools to build anything anywhere, anytime, for any situation you may run into on any given day.

Remember, you do not have to oversee your team to be a builder. You can lead and build from anywhere in the chain of command. While you are navigating this book, I want you to start with your mindset: Believe that growth and knowledge is gained over time and believe in yourself for the long term. You will improve. It's not about the result; it's about the journey. Then, take the tools you now possess and seek out those future builders. Invest the time and energy to mentor them through the early years and tough times. Challenge them to be better, instill in them the mindset and culture of being a builder, and strive to find the cause that's bigger than themselves.

I challenge you to "be a builder" in everything you do everyday.

Part I

THE BUILDER PHILOSOPHY

1

THE DANGER OF LEADING WITHOUT BUILDING

Maybe you are like me: a very driven person who wants to get things done. It's one of my biggest strengths. When there is a challenge, I will drive through the challenge at all costs to accomplish the task. That also makes it one of my biggest weaknesses. When I get in that "at all costs" mindset, I forget about those around me, and that drive pushes people away. I'm sure that if you think about it, you have been in that situation with your strengths. But maybe you are not like me; maybe you are naturally detail-oriented—which is a great strength to have, but under pressure you may overanalyze and take too long to make a decision. Maybe you are more social and bring the team together, yet under stress you may be too concerned about everyone's feelings and not make the tough call. Under pressure we always go back to our comfort zone. That's when being a builder can help you navigate your natural tendencies.

Many people say you need to lead from the front or lead by example. This is true. It gives the people around you an example to emulate as they are learning to lead. However, when you take it to the extreme, this is not effective. If you do everything for the people around you, the inspiration on your team fades away over time. This is exactly what I did when I started my career. No one could do it better or faster than

I could. At least that's what I thought. Looking back, my most trusted friends and colleagues now make a joke that my drive is my biggest strength and my biggest weakness. I always was driven to get the task done instead of coaching and building a team for the long term. I was very selfish and shortsighted.

If you love leading from the front and leading by example, you may be experiencing the downfalls as I did, or you may not have experienced them just yet. But you will. If you like to lead from the middle or the back, you may experience similar issues. Being too involved or not involved enough is a chronic problem.

You must lead by building those around you. You must adapt to the situation and lead from the front, middle, or rear. Provide opportunities to allow those around you to experience the situation and grow from it. Allow the building blocks to slowly stack over time. Your people will have failures; they will not be as fast or as knowledgeable as you, but with the steps, they will develop over time. Whether you are standing next to them or observing from afar, always be there for your team.

In 2006 the world hit me hard and gave me a wakeup call that I was leading too far out front, making everyone around me mad. I couldn't see it. It was the first time I realized that leadership is more than leading from the front or by example. I had to build those around me. I had to be a builder.

While you will later see in depth explanations the best leaders you know built something in you that you are still using today, for this moment, I want to give you an example of what leadership and management can be like if you do not embrace the philosophy of being a builder. It was a major failure in my life and something I still work on today.

Charging the Hill without Your Team

I was at a low point in the mid-2000s, and I had to make a change. I had some good friends and mentors that finally got through to me, and you will hear the stories of my struggles, challenges, and successes throughout the book. They are stories that changed my mindset, and I believe they will put you on the path to being a builder.

On the strong recommendation of my boss (yes, this was my last chance), I started listening to podcasts, going to seminars, and reading books to learn how to minimize stress and frustration when facing challenges and conflict. Maybe you're experiencing the frustration of people not performing or the stress of conflict when things don't go as planned. You are constantly working longer hours, making phone calls to motivate others or chew them out. You are physically doing everything you can all by yourself to get things done, and nobody sees it like you do. You are probably asking the same questions I was:

- "Why do I have to do their job?"
- "Why do I have to remind them all the time?"
- "Why can't they perform?"
- "Don't they know they are making me look bad in front of my boss?"

It was just after lunch when Tim called and wanted to see me in the home office. His normally calm demeanor was not present this time. The 15-minute drive seemed like an hour.

Tim Marsh was my supervisor, mentor, and second dad. We worked together side by side for 24 years. I met Tim in 1992 when he took over as project manager on a hospital project in Visalia, California, where I was a project administrator. From that day on, he coached and mentored me. Over the years, we both grew. He took over as president of the company, and I had moved up to be a project executive for this particular project.

I did not get these kinds of calls but a handful of times over my first 15 years.

I had a feeling it had something to do with the fact that I had been butting heads with the architect and inspector for the last couple of weeks. But I knew what I was doing was right and had to stand my ground. The inspection team did not understand the pressure that a 130 million-dollar project brings to the project executive. I had a staff of 12 people, 60 bid packages in 10 phases on a 530,000-square-foot project that needed to be completed in less than 30 months. This was a Clovis Unified School District project, someone we had been working with for years. The inspection team did not understand that we had to keep moving forward at all costs and they were the ones slowing down the project. The subcontractors did not understand how crucial it was to hit their dates. My key staff members—Cole, Joe, Brady Rex, and Mandie—were working their assess off, and for what? Just to have the architect and inspector kill the momentum? At the time, I just wanted what was best, and I could not fail. This was the largest single school project ever constructed in the state of California, and it all rested on my shoulders.

As I walked into Tim's office, he had an uncharacteristically firm look on his face as he asked me to sit down.

I said, "Man, Tim, what's up?"

"Well," Tim said, "I just got a call from the inspector, and he has requested that you be removed from the project."

"He can't do that!" I yelled. "He's the one with the issue, and I'm busting my ass to get the work done. I'm not the problem—he is!"

Tim sat in silence for what seemed like an eternity, then said, "Doug, you see the challenges and where the project needs to go. You are right."

I said, "Thank you."

He continued, "But sometimes being right and driving so hard is not the best approach. Do you really think the architect and the inspector are trying to make the project fail?"

"It sure seems like it."

He looked at me with a startled look.

"OK . . . no, I don't think they are doing it on purpose," I said. "They have always tried to do the right thing and keep the project moving, so why aren't they doing it now? This is too important to me."

"To you?" Tim asked.

"Yes, my career is riding on this. You put me in charge, and I must lead the charge up the hill, just like you have always taught me. I want my family to be proud. I want you to be proud, and I want my team to be proud."

He said, "Doug, that's a lot of I's. So, *you're* charging the hill, huh?"

"Yes, every single day!"

Tim continued, "Turn around and look down that hill and tell me what you see."

I said, "What do you mean? The hill is just a figure of speech."

"Yes, it is, but it is real," he said. "From where I'm sitting, you are charging the hill, stronger and faster than anyone, and that is the problem. But when I look down the hill, I see the inspector, the architect, the owner, and your team still standing at the bottom. Doug, they are not following you up the hill. Your ideas are great; you can see the problem and the goal, but you are not building confidence and trust in your team so they want to follow you."

That statement hit me like a ton of bricks.

I loved my team. But my drive to make it happen was holding them back.

"Doug, it's not about you. It's all about the project. That's what you need to focus on. You must think, *What would a builder do?*"

"What do you mean, a builder? I'm in the office. I'm not a carpenter."

"No, Doug, not a carpenter—a *builder*. They are remarkably similar. A carpenter takes raw materials, reads the plans, and assembles the materials into something that serves a new purpose. I need you to do that with your team. Build consensus, build trust, and build relationships. You are not one right now, but that's what you need to be: a *builder*," Tim explained.

I said, "OK, Tim, I will do my best."

As the saying goes, it is always darkest before dawn. Over the next few months, instead of things getting better, they started to spiral. Little did I know, the incident with the inspector was just the beginning. My family, friends, coworkers, and trade partners were all disappointed in me and my actions in all parts of my life.

Looking back now, I only wanted what was best for everyone around me. I was going to make it happen myself; I didn't need anyone to help me. But I was wrong. Instead of building trust and long-lasting relationships, my actions did exactly the opposite. No one trusted me, wanted to work with me, or believed

> It was the lowest point in my life, and I had to make a change.

I had their best interests in mind. To top it off, my wife, Jodi, wanted a divorce. I wasn't drinking or going out with the guys; I was working, trying to support my family. But as Jodi told me, even when I was home, I was not home. I was always focused on what I had to do because no one else understood. Just providing financial support was not what my family needed. I needed to be there to support them in life.

It was the lowest point in my life, and I had to make a change. It was at this time that Tim's words rang loud in my ears. I had to be a *builder*. I had to build trust, build relationships, build faith, and build confidence—and I had to start from square one by working on myself first and then on everyone around me.

It was not a short-term fix; this had been going on for years, and it would take years to repair the damage and change my own mindset.

I started with a lot of self-reflection and apologies to everyone around me. I had to change my mindset. I had to be a builder in everything I would do, every day, with everyone around me.

Looking back, Jodi, Tim, Cole, Joe, Brady Rex, and Mandie—as well as the Clovis unified team and numerous trade partners—gave me a second chance and the time to build a new reputation. It took years, but with their support, the philosophy worked.

Tools for Your Toolbox

Each of us has a unique personality trait that we use when leading or solving problems. You may be driven or passive, neither of which is better than the other. As you saw in the story above, under pressure, in a leadership role, your strength can also be your weakness. That means something that is an excellent quality can be exaggerated and elevated to a point that it becomes detrimental to the team. Both are good, but in excess both can become negatives.

Sometimes you can step back, reflect, and see it yourself. Sometimes it may take someone from the outside to give you a different perspective. The point is that for you to be the most effective leader possible, you must be able to analyze constructive criticism and decide what needs to be built to become more effective in the future. It is not a short process. Realize that it will take time to make changes and build your path step-by-step.

Traditionally, being a builder means being a "craftsman," always considering production, the materials, and the quality of the final product. A builder is laser-focused on the problem at hand and how they need to build their part of the project. That is a good thing to accomplish their task. As a leader you must be able to take the issues that arise and place them on the table for all to see and work on together. I missed that concept early in my career. I was taking every issue as my own and blaming others for not performing to my expectations. As you detach from the issue and listen to your team, it gives you a great perspective on the multitude of opportunities for potential solutions. Remember, placing blame will drive your team to their corner and make them feel as though they must defend their position. Building a solution together with collaboration will bring the team together to find the most effective path forward.

Being a builder in everything you do involves qualities that go beyond the task at hand. To be a builder means to build:

trust | consensus | relationships | discipline | confidence | knowledge | health

Those things will live on forever in the people you meet.

If you are building a new team, your team members are the raw materials. You need to build skill and trust. If you are solving a problem, you need to build data or information as well as consensus. If you are struggling personally, you may need to build a unique perspective, knowledge, or even faith in yourself.

There will always be challenges and gaps you must span. It is your job as a leader to build the bridge of consensus, confidence, faith, or relationships to bring the team together to charge the hills together.

As a mentor, Tim saw himself as a builder at that moment. He saw the many things I was doing right and my potential. He had been there himself, and someone had helped him when he was younger. He also pointed out the places I needed to improve. A builder must tell the kind truth even if it may cause conflict in the short term. It will be effective in the long term. That means embracing conflict and kindly telling yourself or the people around you what they need to do differently to be more effective and impactful for the situation.

I, on the other hand, only saw the things I thought I was doing right and did not see what I was doing wrong and the effect I was having on those around me. It was one simple concept but so hard to do. Maybe you are struggling with the same thing. Your strength can also be your weakness.

The idea of being a builder for yourself and for others is to be able to step back and see a distinct perspective, to truly know where you are and be able to look at the problem in pieces to see what is missing. When you feel frustrated, it's a go-to mindset to realize that you can make things happen; it may just take a bit longer than you would like right now. Implement a plan to redirect and build for the future. You need to build the tools, the approach, and the words. You need to make yourself more knowledgeable, more technical, and more approachable to be able to solve the hardest challenges you encounter.

The Tools

1. Under pressure, your strength can also be your weakness. Take a step back and realize the impact you are having on your team.
2. Blaming others is detrimental to building a solution. Put the problem on the table and work on it together.
3. Being open to hear all possibilities to drive collaboration, trust, and success. Be humble and listen to learn. Then make the call.
4. Tell the kind truth to yourself and others. While it will be difficult in the short term, the result in the long term will be success.

2

THE CONSTRUCTION PROCESS AND THE CONSTRUCTION MINDSET

The construction industry is one of the most complex industries on the planet. It is one of the only industries that requires thousands of people from hundreds of companies across the country to build one unique building. From the procurement of raw materials, fabrication, assembly, and shipping, to the coordination of the crews on-site and installation, the coordination and communication required to pull this off is mind-blowing. While there is a general process, every building is unique and has never been built before. Even building the same building on a different site will bring new and unforeseen challenges.

While there are general processes and standards in the industry, teams must be ready to step back, review, and adapt to keep the project moving forward.

The purpose of this chapter is to give you insight into the iterative and unpredictable process of construction. Just like building a building, building relationships, trust, and consensus is also an unpredictable and iterative process. It takes energy and hard work to build and maintain them over time. If you think back, the best teams, relationships, and solutions did not form immediately; it was a process of successes and failures that made them strong and effective.

Think of the solutions and the relationships as you would a building project. You first need a strong foundation to be able to build a structure that will stand the test of time. You must take the raw materials and mold them into something that will be trusted and successful just as a carpenter would with lumber for a wall. As you navigate the rest of the chapter, I challenge you to see the similarities of construction and how it can be a blueprint for you to build relationships, consensus, solutions, and teams.

An Overview of the Three Phases of the Construction Process

First, imagine you are an architect, and you have a vision for a building. You must take that vision and build it on paper (blueprints) with the use of numerous lines, arcs, and angles to convey your vision to the contractor.

> When you are a builder, you will have an impact on everyone around you.

Second, put yourself in the place of the many craftspeople who must look at those lines, order and fabricate materials, and put them together to physically create the building envisioned by the architect.

Finally, imagine yourself as the person who will use the building to transform your community through the services you will provide.

In short: The architect builds a vision (the design), the contractor builds the project (the building), and the owner builds the community. The point, as you may have guessed, is that everyone can be a builder no matter what role they play in the process. When you are a builder, you will have an impact on everyone around you.

Building the Vision

Craftspeople in the construction industry take raw, unorganized material and create systems by using tools, planning, problem solving, and teamwork.

For example, a carpenter will take raw 2x4s, cut them into different lengths, nail them in specific configurations, and create a wall for a structure. Electricians take rolls of wire, bundles of conduits, and stacks of boxes and create a power system for the building. Roofers combine building paper, asphalt shingles, and nails to create a watertight line of defense from weather and rain. The general contractor is responsible for taking these trades and many more and coordinating them all into a complete working structure for you to live, work, or worship.

To be effective, the construction crew must have blueprints that show the vision, the ability to communicate, and the skill to decipher challenges to bring the project together. They are the boots on the ground implementing the vision every day. Construction workers must accomplish all of this while braving extreme weather conditions, safety hazards, and the uncertain market of material deliveries. Next in line to the military and first responders, construction workers have one of the most dangerous and demanding jobs on the planet.

There Is Never a Perfect Project

Construction projects follow a structured sequence of activities over a set period of time. While the exact steps may vary depending on the project type, size, and complexity, certain fundamental stages can be identified. Each step builds upon the previous ones—foundation, structure, infrastructure, and finishes—leading to the creation of a complete building.

The act of constructing a building or infrastructure is rarely linear or straightforward. It entails a series of interdependent tasks that demand coordination between various stakeholders, including architects, engineers, contractors, and craftsmen. It requires the precise sequencing of activities, attention to detail, and constant evaluation of progress. Much like placing the pieces of a puzzle, every decision and action during construction must align with the broader vision, ensuring a cohesive and structurally sound outcome. The process involves multiple interlocking elements that must fit together harmoniously. Each stage of the construction process represents a puzzle piece, contributing to the overall picture and functionality of the final product.

Due to the nature of construction, you must acknowledge that perfection will never be achieved. Rather, it emphasizes the importance of repeated cycles of planning, execution, evaluation, and refinement. Each iteration offers an opportunity to learn, adapt, and improve, bringing the project closer to its desired form.

By recognizing the step-by-step process of construction, professionals can better navigate the complexities and uncertainties inherent in their field. It allows for adjustments to be made along the way, accommodating unforeseen challenges, and incorporating new insights. This iterative mindset encourages collaboration, innovation, and continuous improvement, fostering a culture of learning and adaptability within the construction industry.

The Puzzle

Picture yourself with your family gathered around the table one evening after dinner.

On the table sits a box with a picture on it with the words *one thousand pieces*. I loved doing puzzles with my parents and now with my kids, and when I think back, the process of doing a puzzle is remarkably like construction and similar to solving most challenges in life.

You tear off the plastic on the box, take off the lid, and carefully place it where everyone can see the picture. Then you unceremoniously dump all the pieces on the table.

Now, this is not the 10-piece puzzle from when you were three years old. That would be easy. A 10-piece puzzle takes little planning or preparation because you can see all the pieces at one time. But as the puzzles get bigger, more preparation is needed to be able to bring the pieces together.

You know it's a puzzle. You know what it's supposed to look like, but all the pieces are in chaos scattered across the table, and some of the pieces are even upside down. Now it's your job to dig in and provide the energy to bring the puzzle pieces to complete organization and order.

How do you approach it? Do you jump in and randomly put pieces together? Or do you prepare by looking at the picture, studying what it looks like, sorting through the pieces, forming a strategy, and finding one piece at a time until you can form small groups?

As a kid, you were taught to turn all the pieces over, find the corners, find the edges, orient the corners and edges to connect, then fill in the middle. As you got older, the puzzles became more complex. Some areas got trickier because several areas looked similar in shape and color. But the process was the same: corners, edges, patterns, fill in the middle. The last variable was that everyone sitting around the table had a unique perspective and could add value by seeing things from a unique perspective.

You start seeing patterns and clumps of pieces that fit with other clumps. In no time, you have 99% of the puzzle completed. Then you're looking for that last piece—the one your brother put in his lap so he can finish the puzzle while you are looking on the floor. (Well, that's what my brother did to me.) Once you're done, you break down the puzzle and put it back into the box. When you decide to do the puzzle again in the future, I can guarantee it will not go together in the same way as it did the first time. You will have different challenges, even though it's the exact same puzzle.

Tools for Your Toolbox

Theodore Roosevelt said, "Nothing in the world is worth having or worth doing unless it means effort, pain, difficulty. . . . I have never in my life envied a human being who led an easy life."[1]

Whether you are building a construction project or consensus on a team, there will be challenges, and it will take a lot of energy and collaboration to be successful. It's your job to direct that energy and build a collaborative culture in your team. You will get frustrated at the differing points of view and arguments.

That's where following a process and having a builder's mindset will help you. You know there will never be a perfect project, team solution, or relationship. It's not about the destination; it's about the journey. The journey is following the process and getting as close to perfection as possible.

To be a builder, you must put energy into everything you do. It will be hard. You will say, "Why can't everything go smoothly? or "Why am I doing their job for them?" or "I'm tired of helping them; I have my own work to do." It's OK to be frustrated; you're human. I'm not saying you should do everyone's job for them. I am saying that you should put energy into your work and the people around you. Focus on the incremental successes and wins. Focus on what you can do. Keep your eye on the cause bigger than yourself, and you will be rewarded in the long term.

For the same reason, if you realize that things are not as you had perceived them to be, you must change your perspective and adapt.

---

[1]   Theodore Roosevelt, Address to the Iowa State Teacher's Association, Des Moines, Iowa, 1910.

Let's go back to the puzzle example for a minute. I'm sure sometimes you got frustrated or stumped and had to walk away from the puzzle to clear your head. As the picture formed, you may have turned the puzzle for a new perspective, asked for help to gain new insight, thought *What if*, and tried different things.

In the end, you learned that as challenging as the puzzle looked in the beginning, all the pieces were there, and they fit. With preparation, a good process, a change in perspective, and the ability to adapt, you can bring your unique puzzle together. There's no way to cheat a puzzle—it's a long-term game with no quick solutions or life hacks.

The aim of the rest of this book is to show you that whether you are building a puzzle or a structure, the principles that are used are the same principles required to build relationships, trust, knowledge, stability, and faith. There is no easy way. It takes time, diligence, listening, planning, preparing, deciding, changing perspective, acting in increments, and then adapting. All of this takes discipline and energy to accomplish. You will see the tools it takes to make it happen for you and those around you. In the next chapter, I give an example of a construction issue that describes these principles.

The Tools

1. There is never a perfect project, team, solution, or relationship. It is your job to build and adapt as a leader.
2. It takes energy and collaboration to succeed. When you put in the energy, you will be successful for your team in the long term.
3. This is a long-term game. There are no quick solutions or life hacks. Stick with it and build.
4. Focus on what you can do. Always look for one more thing you can do to move things forward incrementally.

3

BUILDING IS THE MOST IMPORTANT TOOL YOU HAVE IN YOUR TOOLBOX

Now that you understand the approach for construction projects, let's apply those lessons to being a builder. Building is the most used tool in great leaders', managers', and coaches' toolboxes, and it will allow you to create success, rebound from failure, address challenges, and sustain excellence over your career. Building is all around you, not only in the physical sense but also in the metaphorical sense. Of course, you see building projects, roadwork, high-rises, and houses as you drive through the streets of your town every day. But while we will use examples of actual construction techniques to illustrate how to be a builder, I want you to focus on the building of people, ideas, concepts, solutions, and core values that will allow you to have an impact on people and processes around you.

Your first experience with the word *build* was probably playing with building blocks when you were young. Sitting cross-legged on the floor, you probably had about 10 blocks with colored numbers and letters scattered on the floor. You would take them one by one and stack them on top of one another. Then you'd knock them down and do it all over again. Over time, you got more blocks and started stacking them in different configurations. I'll bet you were so proud of your accomplishment.

As kids, we all had the builder mindset and used it all the time.

- Learning to walk and falling? Dust yourself off, get back up, and try again.
- Riding a bike and falling off? Get back on the bike and start pedaling again!
- Learning your ABCs? You did not start with memorizing all 26 letters. You learned three or four and added more each day until you learned them all and could sing the song.
- Learning your numbers? Counting to 10 was the goal, then 20, 30, and 40.

Instead of those things, now as an adult and a leader, you are building much more complex things like teams, ideas, culture, sustainability, and relationships. Yes, sometimes you will make mistakes or maybe even fail just like when you were younger. However, unlike when we were kids, as adults we fear mistakes and see failure as a tragedy. We even avoid the word *failure* for fear of looking bad. You need to get that builder mindset back and see failure as an opportunity to learn and begin again with more knowledge.

For example, good relationships are built over time, not with deals. Building a relationship is an iterative process just like building a structure. You must build a strong foundation. It starts with a small conversation, working through a problem, and meeting your commitments. If that happens consistently over an extended period, trust is built and the relationship grows; the structure of that relationship is strong. Now, there will be struggles, failures, and disagreements. If you can work through those things together, your relationship will stand the test of time. To prove the point, you have all seen shoddy construction where the plaster cracks, the roof leaks, and the paint fades after a short time. The building was built with shortcuts and inferior materials to get a quick result and a quick sale for a short-term gain.

For the same reason, if you rush into a relationship and avoid conflict, the hard discussions, and the questions about philosophy and culture, the relationship is likely to fall apart very quickly.

A True Test of Culture

I was on a project in 2010 when there was a major issue with the color of cabinets that had been delivered to the job site. The project had been going very well. We enjoyed collaborating with the architect and client very much and felt we had a strong relationship. But this issue had the potential to test that relationship. It also had the potential to delay the project, which meant the kids coming back from summer vacation would not have their three science rooms available. The issue at hand was a mistake on the color of the cabinets.

The project was on a large high school campus with multiple science wings. There were many areas that were not going to be modernized, including only some of the cabinets in each room, so they had to be protected from damage during construction. As the drawings called for, the cabinet contractor reviewed the existing cabinet color noted in the drawings and the actual color in the field and then provided samples for review. We, as the contractor, confirmed that the colors matched as well and sent them to the architect for approval. The architect confirmed and approved the samples as a match, and the product was ordered.

On schedule, the cabinets were fabricated, arrived on-site, and were placed in the classrooms for installation. The first wing was installed and went very smoothly. As the installers moved to the second wing and removed the protective coverings, it became clear that the existing cabinets were not the same color as the new cabinets.

How could this be? Well, the campus had originally been built in phases, and there had been many modernizations to parts of the campus. Normally, all science classrooms are built at one time, and no one thought to check all three classrooms to confirm the color.

The fact that three different entities missed the color difference, including the owner who had done an intensive review of the drawings before the bid, was not an excuse. We had to make it right for the school district. We had four weeks to come up with a plan and implement the fix before the students returned to class.

To the credit of the subcontractor, architect, and field team, no one pointed fingers. Everyone knew there would be a huge cost to fix the cabinet color. The team immediately called a meeting with the architect, cabinet contractor, and painter. They discussed many different solutions and considered the time and cost for each.

They decided the best solution for the project was to remove the existing finish and apply the new finish. The painter would take the lead, and the costs would be tracked on a time-and-material basis. While it was a bit more expensive, it was the only solution that would be completed in time for school to start.

During the implementation of the fix, we had a few meetings to discuss responsibility and how to avoid this type of thing in the future. The final cost was just over $125,000. We ended up splitting the costs in four ways according to depth of responsibility.

The relationships and trust we built over the previous five years allowed the team to come together and take responsibility for what they could have done better. No one ran to their corner; instead, we came together and built a solution. That event is still talked about today as a pivotal moment in our relationship. Going forward, we trusted one another more and had faith that everyone would do the right thing for the project (a cause bigger than ourselves).

Building Has Always Been a Part of Success

The word *build* is used millions of times every day around the world. It's a universal term that means to take something that is disorganized and bring the pieces together to create something that can serve a purpose that could not be achieved before.

For example, Erin Brockovich had to build a case to help the people getting sick from underground water in their town. Presidents have had to build a platform for their campaign to convey ideas to their constituents. Sales managers must build a team to communicate with their clients, and you must build a culture in your company and your family.

Sometimes people will use the word *rebuild*. For example:

- "We need to rebuild our relationship."
- "We need to rebuild that house after the fire."
- "After the war in the Middle East, the president declared they would "rebuild their nation."

You have probably experienced a relationship that has deteriorated. The solution is to build. The relationship may need to build trust. The team may need to build consensus.

Pause for a moment and try to remember a great manager who organized and implemented processes that made your team more effective. They knew how to be a builder—building processes, trust, and effectiveness to realize a specific goal.

Now, think about a great leader in your life who provided a vision for work, life, family, or religion. They had special qualities that gave you the inspiration to follow them. They built a vision, consensus, and inspiration to move you toward a goal.

As you think back on your life, you may have had a favorite teacher, or a coach who helped you through a struggle. Did they build knowledge, understanding, stamina, or skill in your life? Maybe a boss held you to a high standard that you didn't understand at the time but now realize he built tenacity, diligence, and discipline to make you more successful in your life.

All the great managers, coaches, and leaders were also great builders. John F. Kennedy announced the goal of going to the moon. He did it in a speech at Rice University where he declared, "We choose to go to the moon in this decade and do the other things, not because they are easy, but because they are hard."[2]

Kennedy did not stop with the vision; he built teams, built trust, built confidence, built perseverance, and built discipline into the very organization that was tasked with this incredible feat. There were massive setbacks and schedule delays, technical failures, and discouraged team members. Had he stopped with the vision and just ruled with an iron fist to get the job done, the astronauts would not have made it to the moon. Instead, he continued to build a belief in his team that the mission could be carried out and that allowed his team to persevere through trying times. On July 20, 1969, the United States achieved Kennedy's goal of putting a man on the moon.

Builders focus on what they have in common and then work out the things they don't to come to a consensus for a cause that everyone can get behind. You may not get it 100% your way, but you will build, learn, and grow.

Tools for Your Toolbox

Think of the word *build* as a tool that has been used to bring people together and solve great challenges. In each of the examples above, the leader used building as a tool. It took an immense amount of energy, teamwork, and fortitude to get the results they did. In fact, they made history, as each of their successes stands as an example for us today.

In each case, they knew where they were, and they had a goal of where they wanted to be. They had to build something to get them there—information, technology, a message, engineering, or a team.

You have heard the saying "You have to build a bridge" hundreds of times. I'm going to show you how important that saying is in your

---

[2]   John F. Kennedy, Address at Rice University on the Nation's Space Effort, September 12, 1962, https://www.jfklibrary.org/learn/about-jfk/historic-speeches/address-at-rice-university-on-the-nations-space-effort.

everyday lives. Whether you are building a bridge to another person for a relationship or consensus or building a bridge to do something that has never been done before, like going to the moon, you always must build something to get you there.

The question you need to ask yourself is: "What material do I need to use to build that bridge?" It could be empathy with someone who is struggling. It could be information if you are trying to gain consensus. It could be confidence when someone doesn't think they can do it. It could be technology to go to the moon.

Builders are successful in what they do because they are humble, driven, take the time to understand the situation and people around them, and build solutions for a cause bigger than themselves. When you build, step back and figure out the gap—the type of bridge you need—and start building it. Once you get everyone across the bridge standing next to one another, you can move forward toward the cause that's bigger than themselves.

To sustain excellence over time, you must build. Build trust, consensus, relationships, sustainability, discipline, confidence, knowledge, financial stability, and much more. Building will allow you to reach your goals.

The Tools

1. You must always build something to get to your goal. As the leader, step back and ask yourself, "What do I need to *build?*"
2. Focus on what you have in common and build consensus on that. This will allow you to continue to build a team that is aligned going forward.
3. To sustain excellence over time, you must build. It takes energy and diligence, and you can provide that leader to take your team to the next level.

4

"YOU ARE HERE"—KNOW WHERE YOU ARE AND WHERE YOU WANT TO BE

You've probably been to a mall, walked up to a kiosk with a directory and map, and noticed the big red dot that says "You Are Here." Seeing that dot gives you a frame of reference of where you are in the mall. As a part of the map, there is also a directory of the shops with a number next to each shop. At a single glance you can see the big picture and the detailed picture of your situation. If you want to find a shoe store, you look through the directory for your store, find the corresponding number on the map, then trace the path through the mall from the dot to your store. This is something you do almost naturally.

So why is it so hard to apply "You Are Here" to more complicated issues like finding a solution to relationships or challenges at work? It's because you don't have all the information. You can't stand in front of a board to see the whole picture and make a call. You need to gather more information to be able to make the best decision on the path to take to where you want to go.

A simple example is playing poker. You know where you are with the cards in your hand. You know where you want to be: winning the pot of money. The problem is that you don't know what cards the other players have in their hand. The solution is to gather information by placing bets, gauging reactions, and deciding if you should continue. It all plays out as calculated risks, and you may or may not win based on actual information or deceit in the form of bluffs.

When you apply the builder philosophy to relationships and challenges, you have a process to follow to gain information that gives you a better understanding of the situation so you can make the best decisions possible for the outcome of a cause bigger than yourself. Bill Walsh, author of *The Score Will Take Care of Itself*, states that when you do the right things and implement the process, you will succeed. Put in the work and the score will take care of itself. It is the same with being a builder. Trust the process of building and you will get where you want to go.

Let's look at a more complicated example: a road trip. Unlike when you were younger, you now use an app on your phone to find directions to your destination. You first put in your location (where you are), then enter your destination (where you want to be). The third step is "get directions." Within two seconds, the app has found three routes for you to select and shows the duration of the trip for each. You pick the route and select go. The entire process takes less than 60 seconds.

Over the past 15 years, our society has moved toward the expectation of a quick fix and a quick solution for everything we do. But there are some things in this world that just take time if you want to get the best result. Mapping apps are a notable example of how technology has improved our lives. They calculate how traffic is building, slowing, or flowing. They consider detours, accidents, and roadblocks and calculate new routes on the fly. But the premise of what they are doing in the background is the foundation of what it means to be a builder. Just the process of reading an old-school paper map will provide insight into what you need to do to be a builder every day in everything you do.

For the next few chapters, I'll take things back to the basics and give examples of how to slow down and follow a process for facing challenges and solving problems. As I said before, there is no fast way to gain knowledge, get in shape, or create a strong relationship. You must put in the work to build a strong process, then repeat it every day; over time you will see the results.

Fishing Trip

My dad taught me to read a map before our fishing trip when I turned thirteen. The story is simple, but it applies so much to the things we do every day.

My dad and I had been fishing in lakes and ponds with a pole, a bobber, and a chair for as long as I could remember. Fun family times, great discussion, fresh air . . . but not much activity. I had been asking for years to fish on a river so we could cast, reel, and walk up and down the river to find the best spot. My dad's standard answer was, "You're not old enough; we'll go when you turn 13." Now, I was a persistent kid and that didn't stop me from asking over and over, but my dad was persistent too, and every time I got the same answer.

However, another quality of Dad's was that he was true to his word. So, for my 13th birthday, he got me a new rod and reel, a tackle box, and brand-new lures! In the card, he wrote, "Happy Birthday, Doug; be ready to leave at 4:00 a.m. Saturday. We are going fishing on the Merced River!" I was beyond excited. I shouted, "Thank you! I will be ready!" and gave him a huge hug.

My dad got home from work on Friday, and over dinner we talked about the trip. As my mom was cleaning up, my dad went into the other room and came back with a neatly folded map.

He said, "Sit down with me, Doug. I want to show you how to read a map."

He gently unfolded the map and spread it on the table.

He asked, "Do you know where we are on the map?"

I looked at the maze of lines and colors and pointed to the only thing I could recognize—Fresno—and said, "Fresno! We are in Fresno."

He said "Good job! Now, can you tell me where we live in Fresno?"

I looked and looked, but all I could see was the maze; nothing made sense.

He said, "Do you remember when we used to do puzzles? This, like anything else you do for the first time, is just like a puzzle. It seems overwhelming at first, but it will get simpler as you do it over and over. You must be able to remember and apply the knowledge from the previous experiences."

My dad smiled and said, "The first thing you need to be able to do is find where you are so you know where you are starting from."

He started with north, south, east, and west and then showed me how the map was broken into blocks of 1000. We were on the 4600 block of North Fisher. He led me through the numbers 4300, 4400, 4500, and 4600. I said, "That's our block!" I slid my finger into the corner where we lived. It was so easy to see now. I could see the streets, the schools I went to, where my friends lived—all of it was clear.

Then my dad said, "OK, where are we going fishing?"

"The Merced River!" I said.

"OK, find it on the map."

I could see the lakes and the mountains. I knew the Merced River was in the mountains. After that, I just stared. The 1000 block thing I had just learned didn't help me at all. So, my dad started with something I knew. He said, "Here is Millerton Lake." We went fishing there a lot. It was blue with thin blue squiggly lines coming out of it.

He then said, "The blue squiggly line is the San Joaquin River." We had driven past that many times on the way to Millerton. He slid his finger up to another blue squiggly line, and there I saw the words *Merced River.*

"So, how do you think we should get there?" Dad asked.

There were a million roads between our house and the river. Every time I thought I understood and was getting the hang of the map, the next step was right back to the state of confusion.

My dad said, "Just like the puzzle, let's take it one step at a time." He walked me along the route on the freeway, as well as a couple of back-road routes. We sat and talked about which route would be the quickest and the most scenic. We finally decided to take the freeway there and the country roads on the way back.

The morning came, and we got into his 1978 El Camino; we had lunch, snacks, sodas, fishing poles, and tackle box. As we pulled out of the driveway, I followed the streets on the map with my finger and told him every turn to make. I was proud of myself, and he was proud of me.

The fishing trip was better than I could have expected. We both caught fish, and we talked to a ranger who was checking for licenses. He was a nice guy and excited for me. That night we cleaned the fish and ate them for dinner. It's an experience I will always remember.

As I look back, I realize how far technology has come and how much we are missing in the process of reading a map. Today we put the destination into our phone and start from our current location. We have satellite imagery that shows the buildings around us, gas stations, restaurants, and hotels. The tool has evolved to do all the calculations for us in less than two seconds. It gives us alternate routes and arrival times and will even change routes based on traffic.

Our phones now do all the things we would have done with a map and more, but we never see the process; it's instantaneous.

But not everything in our life can be instantaneous. You are not Google or Waze in every aspect of your life. You cannot train for a marathon in a day, you cannot instantly read a book and gain all knowledge, and you cannot instantly lose thirty pounds. These all require a process, just like reading a map. To this day, Dad is a great builder. In this case, he had to build a bridge for the gap in knowledge I had in reading a map. Those types of moments continued throughout my life for music, youth groups, girlfriends, marriage, and kids. Whenever I get wrapped up in wanting things too quickly, I remember the time I sat with my dad to learn how to read a map, slow down, and enjoy the process.

Tools for Your Toolbox

Whether you are building a relationship, a building, or a plan for a trip, knowing where you are and where you want to be is critical when you get into real-life challenges. The mindset of being a builder will help you start in the right direction.

My dad and I figured out where we were on the map, and then found the destination at the Merced River where we wanted to be. In this case, I had never read a map before, so I had to learn from scratch. In business and in life, you may run into situations like this where you must learn something before starting the process.

Let's take a look at an actual issue we had on a project as an example. We are all usually quick to pass judgment based on what we have observed and what we think we know about a situation. I think you'll agree that good decisions are never made in a panic or when you are stressed. When you slow down and open your mind to all possibilities, solutions always bubble to the top.

We had heavy rainstorms that shut down most of our projects for eight weeks straight in 2022. Just as the rain would stop and the site would start to dry out, it would rain again. We had a couple of deadlines that were looming as students were about to come back from winter vacation.

We had removed all the existing walkways and performed the work required when it started raining. The only thing left was to pour back the walkways, and we had started ahead of schedule. All the rain, though, hindered our progress, and now we had just four days to complete the work before students came back to school. This was an especially critical area of the campus, and we could not miss our goal. I scheduled a meeting with the project team, and we started with "where we are" and "where we want to be" to solve the problem.

I asked the superintendent, "Where are we now?"

He said, "We are stopped because of the rain."

I said, "Well, that's not actually where we are; that's the perception of the situation. Think a little more broadly."

He continued, "We have completed all the demolition and all the underground utilities, and we have graded the new walkways. All the walkways are currently flooded, and we cannot pour concrete."

I said, "Good—now we have a good definition of where we are, and we can start to address the issue. So, where do we want to be?"

"We want to have all the walkways poured and ready for the kids no later than four days from today," the superintendent responded.

The team initially thought they were stopped because of the rain. The real problem was that the kids couldn't get to the classrooms. Once we realized this, the team could focus on a different set of solutions. Ultimately, they came up with a blueprint that showed the tasks and the order they could implement them to give the kids a path to the classroom.

To create a blueprint for a solution that will allow you to get where you want to go, you have to start with an accurate, unbiased assessment of where you are. The problem comes when you've had a lot of experience in similar situations. You apply experiences from your past to help fill in the gaps of what is not known to help you make a decision. Your experiences, while valuable, can cloud your perception of the facts of the current situation. To know where you are means to know where you *really* are when you strip away the perceived facts generated by your past experiences. In Chapter 5 you will see real-life examples of how beliefs of where you are can change by talking through the facts and asking your team the right questions.

Where you want to go is the goal, not the path. Defining where you want to be will allow you to create multiple paths to get there. For example, we needed to get kids back to their classrooms. There were many ways to get to the goal:

- We could work overtime to pump water and pour concrete.
- It might stop raining so no pumping would be needed to pour concrete.
- The principal could relocate the classrooms until the walkways were poured and the kids could return.

There are always options to get to your goal. You must establish where you want to be to be able to develop the options for getting there.

For now, remember that your perception is your reality, but it may not be the real situation. Ask questions, be diligent, and find the best information possible to allow you to make the most effective decisions for your team.

The Tools:

1. Knowing where you are and where you want to be is critical when you get into real-life challenges. These are your starting and ending points.
2. You must start with an accurate, unbiased assessment of where you are. Hope is not a plan. You must have a realistic picture of the situation you are in.
3. Where you want to go is the goal, not the path. There are many ways to get to a goal. The goal is just the place you want to be, not the path you will take to get there.

5

FOUR MINDSETS OF A BUILDER

The Philosophy

When dealing with a frustrating situation, it's normal to vent and place blame. Your mindset is critical when approaching a challenge. The four mindsets of a builder allow you to take a step back and look at a situation from an unemotional standpoint.

1. **Solve the problem.** Focus on the problem itself. Human nature instantly looks for blame; ignores the problem, hoping it will go away; or makes a quick, short-term deal to keep moving forward. The adage "Pay me now or pay me later" applies perfectly to this mindset. Use discipline and diligence to work through the challenge and solve the problem.

2. **Focus on what you can do.** You have probably been in many situations when you were a part of or leading a group that had to solve a problem. For every potential solution, there were probably quite a few people who focused on what they couldn't do or why it wouldn't work. Again, this is natural, so don't let it bog you down. While it's good to note the roadblocks (they do need to be addressed), the only way to solve a problem is to focus on what you can do—even if that means an incremental approach to move toward the solution.

3. **Always be curious.** This is the engine that drives the other
    mindsets. In an emotional state, you want to take charge, lead
    the conversation with what you know, and make decisions
    quickly. Curiosity allows you to check your ego, calm the situa-
    tion, and ask questions to gain information from other people
    with different perspectives that may change the way you look
    at the situation. By using curiosity and the additional informa-
    tion it provides, you can make a more effective decision.

4. **Always improve your situation.** While curiosity is important,
    it must be tempered with action. You have probably heard the
    phrase *paralysis by analysis*. Overanalyzing before you start for
    fear of failure or not having the perfect plan won't improve
    your situation. In the right proportion, analysis improves your
    situation because you have more knowledge. Taking the first
    steps of a plan even though you can't see exactly what the
    final step looks like improves your situation. Taking an incre-
    mental approach allows you to move forward while being
    curious. Getting feedback to make the next decision or action
    is important.

Flight 163—Testing the Four Mindsets

After 25 years of marriage, my wife, Jodi, and I planned a trip to
Ireland. It was a "bucket list" trip. While we had taken numerous trips
over the years, both in and out of the country, this would be our first
major vacation: five days and five nights near a small Irish village called
Maynooth. We were hoping to get to know people, see the sights, golf,
and enjoy the beer and whisky the area was known for.

The day of the trip, we woke up excited at 4:30 a.m. As we prepared to leave, I received a text that our flight had been delayed an
hour and a half. I checked our layover in Toronto and saw that we
would miss our connecting flight.

"Jodi, our flight is delayed," I said. As she looked at me, I continued, "And we will miss our connecting flight."

Both of us stood there as if to say, "This can't be happening."

While we didn't know it at the time, this was only the beginning of the challenges we would face on our journey to Ireland. To make a long story short, we missed connecting flights, airlines had mechanical issues, we sprinted to make flights, and we ended up without our luggage in London and no plan of how to get to Ireland. From Fresno to San Francisco, then to Toronto and finally London, it was quite the adventure.

Both Jodi and I were determined to find a way. Instead of being angry, we went into curiosity mode and asked a lot of questions to find options. We let it be known we were open to other flight options.

When we got to London, we headed for baggage claim. There were 120 people standing in baggage claim at Heathrow, with no airline personnel in sight.

Finally, one man walked up from the secured area and said, "There is no flight to put all of you on. You will be receiving an email or text with your new flight information. If you must stay overnight, save your receipts, and the airline will reimburse you. Thank you."

We were all stunned. No one knew what to do. Some people were angry, some were calm, and most were confused. Everyone was on their phones trying to find new flights. We were stuck in London, which is not a bad place to be stuck, but our phones weren't working to make international calls.

The luggage started coming out onto the belt. As time went on, we didn't see our luggage. Person after person was leaving until we were the last ones standing without luggage, without any email about a flight, and no idea where to turn next. We were close to 30 hours with limited sleep, in a country we had never been to, and without any knowledge of how to navigate the system. The airline representatives said they were sorry but there was nothing they could do until the flight was rescheduled and restated that we would receive an email.

As tired and as frustrated as we were, we looked at each other, took a deep breath, and realized we could not let the frustration ruin our trip. We knew where we were: Heathrow. We knew where we wanted to be: Ireland. Now we had to create a blueprint of how to bridge the gap to get there. We sat down and thought through the problem.

Using the Four Mindsets

Solve the Problem

Our initial reaction was that the airline screwed up and canceled the flight. The mechanical issue was the problem. It would be quite easy to get upset and blame the airline for the problem. Another problem that could be considered is that we missed a day of our trip, while others on the flight missed a wedding or a rugby match. But as we sat there, the real problem was that we didn't have a flight or our luggage, and the *result* was that we would miss a day of our trip.

Many times, we look to the cause as the problem rather than the actual problem that is the result of the cause that needs to be solved. This is a key point to remember when you're emotional and feeling upset or frustrated. You need to take a step back, ask questions, and find the actual problem to be solved.

Focus on What You Can Do

Many times, when you are frustrated, the knee-jerk reaction is to sit and wait for the main problem to be solved. But usually there are many other smaller things that could be happening while the main issue is in the process of being solved or while you're waiting for information.

At this point, we didn't have control over our flight, but the airline was working on it. We had to wait for the email to know the status of our next flight. So, we moved to the next problem. This was the status of our luggage. It was the only thing we could do at the time, and while it was not the most critical, it would become critical very soon. This was the second step in building an overall solution prior to getting to Ireland.

We pulled out our boarding passes with the luggage ticket stubs and moved to the lost luggage counter. A gentleman summoned us to the desk and said, "How can I help you?"

I said, "We were just on flight 163 that was canceled."

He said, "Oh yes, I heard about that, and I'm sorry it was canceled."

I explained, "We were the only ones to not find our luggage on the belt. Could you please look and find out where our luggage may be?"

He said, "Yes, just a moment." After some research, he came back and said, "Your luggage is on flight 169 scheduled to take off later this evening."

I said, "That's strange—we haven't received an email saying we are on flight 169."

He said, "Well, your luggage is on the flight for Dublin tonight."

I said, "OK, can you research if we are on flight 169 from here?"

He said, "No, you'll need to go upstairs to ticketing."

We thanked him and went on our way, hopeful that we had already been assigned a flight but just hadn't received the email. After all, why would they put luggage on a flight and not put the passengers there as well? That question would soon become a new problem to solve.

Through focusing on what we could do, we ended up gaining information about the main issue of our flight. The fact that we hadn't received an email but our luggage was on a flight presented a situation that didn't make sense. Why would this have happened? And that's where we needed to use curiosity and ask more questions instead of just accepting what we had been told.

Always Be Curious

When you're in a tense and unknown situation, curiosity is your friend. It will keep your mind on the goal—learning as much as possible to solve the issue. Normally, as human beings, your first reaction is to point a finger for someone else to solve the problem. You did nothing wrong, so they should solve it to appease you.

Here's another point of view. Do you believe that two heads are better than one? Everyone has different experiences and perspectives. Combining your knowledge and experience can lead to new ideas, questions, and solutions to a problem. Sometimes just talking it through will bring new ideas. For every challenge, there are always questions to ask to drill deeper and find more information.

We headed out of the baggage claim area and up to the fifth level of Heathrow Airport. We were almost giddy that our luggage had been found, and if we had a flight out that night, we would only lose half a day.

As we got to the airline's ticketing counter, we saw 20 people in the general line and one person in the priority line.

We didn't know when our flight was, so Jodi emphatically said, "We are priority today." We both laughed.

We jumped in the line, and I explained the situation to the attendant. She said, "You will need to talk to our supervisor," and pointed to her left.

I said, "Good afternoon, Heather, my name is Doug, and this is Jodi, and I believe we met earlier regarding the flight 163 issue."

She said, "Yes, I remember you. I'm sorry about the situation."

I said, "Thank you, but it sounds like it may have been resolved. We were just down at the baggage claim area, and we found out that our luggage is currently on flight 169. We haven't received an email, but that seems to be a good indicator that we would be on flight 169 tonight. Can you please check?"

She checked her computer screen, and then, with a puzzled look on her face, she checked again. Still puzzled, she looked up at us and said, "You're not on flight 169."

I said, "That's strange, because our luggage is on flight 169. With all the confusion, could it be that our luggage was put on one flight, and we are on another?"

She said, "Let me check." After many clicks of the computer, she cocked her head and said, "I don't have your name on flight 169 or any flight coming up. You're not in the system at all."

Jodi and I looked at each other, and our hearts sank. How could this be? Our initial thought—and we could see it in each other's eyes—is that the airlines had screwed up so badly that we weren't even in the system anymore. What was going on? But we refrained and instead said, "Well, there must be something in the system because we were on flight 163. And our luggage is now on flight 169, so we must be in the system somewhere, right?"

She thought for a minute and said, "Right—let me call someone in baggage."

My mind was racing through the options and the possible questions I could ask to keep the process going. We could tell that Heather had been working there for quite some time and genuinely wanted to solve the problem.

Heather furiously typed in different words and kept trying to find what flight we were on. A surprised look came across her face, and she said, "Well, we found you in the system! You are currently on flight 151 tomorrow morning at 7:40 a.m."

At this point, we were disappointed, but at the same time, we were extremely excited that we were on a flight, even though we still hadn't received an email.

I said, "Heather, thank you so much. I realize you didn't cause this problem, but you've done everything you could to sift through the data and help us solve the problem. How long have you been here at the airline?"

She said, "I started in 1987, and I've been here ever since."

I said, "Heather, you obviously know your job very well, and I appreciate you taking the time to work through the problem with us." She thanked us for being patient, and a small smile came over her face.

Always Improve Your Situation

While we didn't have a flight that night, our situation had improved a bit because, through all of the curiosity and questions, we found we had in fact been booked on a flight. Although slowly, we were making progress by building on one small success after another.

Heather said, "Will you be needing your luggage tonight? Otherwise it can stay on flight 169 and meet you in Dublin tomorrow."

"We will definitely need the luggage," we said in unison. "We are staying in London tonight and we only have our backpacks."

She said, "No problem. I'll see if we can get your luggage pulled from flight 169 and sent back to baggage claim for you." After a few phone calls, she said she had requested that the luggage be returned and we would need to return to baggage claim. "I'll take you down there myself."

Heather led us down through security to the baggage claim area. She told me, "The baggage will be coming out of this chute. And if it doesn't after a little while, go talk to the lost baggage attendants, and they will be able to help you."

I said, "Thank you, Heather," and she was on her way.

Jodi and I sat in silence and bristled with anticipation every time the green light came on and the belt started, but after five deliveries, we still did not have our luggage.

While we were waiting, we decided to look for a hotel to stay in for the evening. As luck would have it, there was a hotel just across the parking garage from terminals two and three, a six-minute walk. That was music to our ears, so I went through the process and booked the hotel.

After a thirty-minute wait, I decided to go down and ask the lost baggage attendants for the status of our bags as Heather had suggested. I spoke to a lovely woman. She took my ticket, scanned the computer, and said, "I have good news for you, three of your four bags came out of chute seven, and they're probably sitting in that cluster of bags right behind you."

I walked over to the cluster of bags and circled the entire area. As I rounded the last corner, I saw all of our luggage! It was a huge relief.

Things were continuing to improve by using the four mindsets.

The Four Mindsets in Action

We wheeled our luggage across the parking garage and into the hotel. We walked up to the counter, and I gave the smiling woman at reception our name and said, "We have a reservation for tonight."

She looked through the computer but couldn't find a reservation. She put in our names again and then said, "Your reservation is for tomorrow night."

I said, "I just booked it an hour ago for tonight."

She asked if I had a receipt, and I pulled up the email. Looking at the email, it was for the next night. I said, "I must have made a mistake in the hurry of putting everything together. Can we get a hotel room for tonight?"

She said, "I'm sorry, sir, but we are completely booked."

I explained our situation and asked if there was anything that could be done, even a spare room that they might hold for emergencies. A supervisor came over and said with a smile, "I'm so sorry, sir, but we are booked up with all the canceled flights; we have no rooms available."

And then, something happened I never would have expected. The supervisor showed that she was a builder too. She had used the four mindsets without even being asked.

The supervisor said, "I heard your conversation, and I've already looked at our sister hotel two minutes from here, and they have rooms available. Would you like us to book a room for you this evening?"

I said, "Yes, please do."

Then, while I was talking to the supervisor, the first person we had talked to, unbeknownst to me, was scheduling a taxi to take us to the hotel. As I finished with the supervisor, the first person walked up and said, "We have a taxi on the way to pick you up. Just wait in the lobby, and he will be in to pick up your luggage."

In a matter of five minutes, the staff at the hotel had used all four mindsets to help take care of us. They focused on what they could do, used curiosity to find a hotel and a car, improved our situation, and solved the problem I had created with my booking mistake.

We made it to our hotel that night, had dinner, and got a good night's rest. The next day, we woke up, got to the airport, had a nice breakfast, boarded the plane, and arrived in Dublin to start our vacation. It was an amazing trip filled with golf, castles, wonderful food, and of course, beer and whiskey. It was a trip we will never forget!

Tools for Your Toolbox

When you're in the middle of a problem and trying to solve it, avoiding the tendency to vent about the situation or blame someone else is sometimes very hard. While it is hard to do, the four mindsets are another tool you can use to take the emotion out of a situation to allow you to think clearly about how to move forward in the most effective manner possible. Start with solving the problem. Remember, what you think is the problem initially may not be the root problem. Give yourself some time and have an open mind about the situation.

Looking back at the story, we could have had the perspective that:

- Our flight was canceled.
- We lost a day of our trip.
- The airlines lost our luggage.
- They didn't have a flight for us.

Our situation had not improved. Complaining about what has happened in the past would have only paralyzed our ability to move forward.

Instead, we looked at it as:

- We now know where our luggage is.
- We do have a flight.

Our situation improved because we focused on what we could do and what we could control. We focused on the small improvements in our situation, thanked people for their help, and kept a positive attitude.

Curiosity is the mindset that will keep you grounded throughout the process. Instead of thinking, *Why is this happening to me?*, change your perspective, be curious, and think, *What is driving the situation and what can I do to have an effect on the next step?* It is hard; you will get emotional. It's disappointing when something does not go as planned. When that happens, bring yourself back to being a builder with curiosity.

Sometimes you must be the one who will improve your situation by communicating, asking questions, and letting people know your situation even if you did not cause the challenge. You can take the initiative to be a builder even if it's not your problem. Had we been upset, frustrated, and blameful toward the airline attendants, they may not have been as inclined to help us. We were standing with them side by side and walking through the process together. As a builder, you can make a positive impact on any situation by solving the problem, focusing on what you can do, always having curiosity, and always moving forward and improving your situation.

The Tools

1. Solve the problem.
2. Focus on what you can do.
3. Always be curious.
4. Always improve your situation.

Part II

THE PROCESS

6

THE "LISTEN PLAN BUILD" PROCESS

In construction, a blueprint shows the architect's vision for a building. Through all the lines and notes, it defines the individual materials that will come together to be the building itself. It provides a clear and concise plan for the project. It is a plan that must be brought to life by many contractors working together toward a common goal. However, in construction as well as in life, even the most well laid-out plan does not always go perfectly. And that, my friends, is why the world needs leaders like you to develop the skills, processes, and mindsets to navigate those challenges.

As I mentioned in the earlier chapters, navigating challenges once came naturally to you. You didn't just learn to walk or build a puzzle. You learned a process to accomplish those things. The process includes watching, trying, failing, and then trying again—a blueprint for learning, failing, and succeeding.

Listen Plan Build is the process for developing a plan and then adjusting that plan when you hit a challenge. It allows you to plan and adapt over and over until you reach your goal. Here is the foundation of what it means.

Listen
Gather information without bias.

Plan
Create tasks or research that needs to be done to formulate a direction to move.

Build
Take action.

The process of Listen Plan Build is specific and tailored to help you overcome challenges. What I have learned over the last 30 years is that there are many ways that do not work. I have failed badly in many areas. Emotions, venting, directness, anger, and sarcasm all used in the wrong way are catastrophic.

You probably know several people whom you consider experts in their field. They have technical knowledge that far surpasses those around them. Excellent leaders "build" to solve problems. The Listen Plan Build process will help you do just that. The by-product of learning to solve problems is that you will gain an immense amount of information while you listen and plan with the experts. Your job as a leader and problem solver is to listen to those around you, put a plan together, and then implement that plan and execute.

As you approach a challenging issue, the first thing you need to remember is that emotions may be running high and motives may differ among your team. It is human nature to be emotional in challenging situations because of personal investment, reputation, or even money that could be lost if something goes wrong. Your job is to first recognize that, then to allow it to happen in a controlled manner.

Listen Plan Build is the process that:

1. Allows people to feel they have been heard
2. Allows people to feel they have contributed to the plan
3. Allows people to take ownership of the actions when implementing the solution

Putting Listen Plan Build into Action

I got a call from one of our project teams. They had been delayed in several areas by the client making changes and by delivery delays. The client's representative had written an email littered with multiple questions and accusations about our performance. The end of a project is always the most stressful. The team had been on the project for over a year, they had worked their butts off, and they were tired and ready to move on to the next project. The approach of hammering the team versus gaining an understanding was not ideal, but it was the hand we were dealt from the owner's representative. The representative had been brought in by the owner with only a few months left in the project. Until that time, we had maintained an excellent relationship. The client realized they needed help in-house to manage all the projects that were under construction and those that were about to start. The rep lacked perspective on the history of the project and came in with hard core approach. We had worked together in the past, and while he did not share our process and philosophy, I knew we could work through the differences.

I visited the job site the next day to meet with the team. When I asked about the issue and how we could best solve the problem, I was met with a barrage of emotional outbursts about how upset they were and how the client rep didn't understand anything. This went on for about 10 minutes as I listened to all their complaints about the situation.

I then calmly asked, "OK, so how do we solve the problem?"

Andrew said, "We can't solve the problem; he's wrong."

"Ok, if he is wrong, why is he wrong? Is he misinformed? Does he know something we don't?"

With a dejected look Andrew said, "I don't know."

I brought the team together in front of the whiteboard. I wrote *LISTEN* at the top of one column, *PLAN* in the next, and *BUILD* in the last column.

LISTEN	PLAN	BUILD

"Whether someone is right or wrong is not what we are trying to solve. We are trying to solve the problem. You as a team need to define the problem. You have been telling me that the client rep is wrong, and you are very emotionally driven right now. Does emotion solve the problem?" I asked.

I continued, "Do you think he wants the project to fail?"

They all shook their heads no.

"Good," I said. "What do we need to build?"

THE "LISTEN PLAN BUILD" PROCESS   53

They said, "What do you mean?"

I answered, "We have a gap in perception and perspective. If a builder was in the field, had a bunch of materials lying on the ground, and found that the wall he was building had some pieces that were not fitting and connecting quite right, what would he build?"

Brent jumped in and said, "He would pull out his measuring tape, remeasure the area, and identify the materials he had in place and the material he had left. Then he would look at the drawings to see what was intended and look for discrepancies. Once he found the problem, he could then come up with a plan to make the right corrections."

I said "Right". So, if each of you was standing on opposite sides of a river and you had to get to the same side, what would you do?"

"Build a bridge," Eddie said.

I said, "Right! So where do we start?"

Listen

"Let's start with the email," Eddie said. "We are going to break down every question and statement. We need to build some understanding on our part first."

We sat together underlining and summarizing the email. Once the highlighting and notes were done, we returned to the whiteboard.

I asked, "What were we doing when we were breaking down the email?"

Andrew said, "Acting like a builder, highlighting, and taking notes."

"RIGHT! But we were doing so much more than that—we were listening."

"Listening?" they said.

"Yes, listening. Guys, listening is about verbal and written clues. Listening is gathering information, just like a builder would do. Listening is a concept. It could be in the contract, the drawings, an email, a meeting, or a one-on-one conversation. You listen to learn and gather information without ego, emotion, or preconceived thoughts."

I then asked, "Where are we?"

Eddie said, "We're mad at the owner's rep," a sentiment echoed by the team.

I said with a smile, "OK, it sounds like you still have some more venting to do."

Eddie responded with, "You're right; it's hard when you're so upset."

I explained they were upset because they had been trying so hard, and they didn't feel like they were being recognized.

Eddie said, "Yeah, but he doesn't even have all his facts right!"

I said, "OK, let's start with where we are, as there is a large misunderstanding. Now, where do we want to be?"

Brent responded this time with, "Off of this job as fast as possible."

I laughed and said, "OK, guys, we are in a tough spot, we have a lot of emotions, and we need to turn that energy into being a builder. Where do we want to be?"

"We want to complete the project, and we want the client to be happy."

I said "Right! So, what is the problem we are trying to solve?"

Eddie said, "I think we need to solve the misunderstanding and get everyone on the same page. It's not as bad as they think it is."

"Right," I said. "We need to build good information that will eventually allow us to build consensus and trust. Venting is a normal part of the project. If you are going to take the lead on being a builder for your team, though, once the venting is done, it is time for you to ask a few questions."

Following the same thread, I moved to the next phase of the process with the team.

I said, "Now that we know where we are, where we want to be, and we know the problem we need to solve, let's start with *LISTEN*."

They were now all in. They could see the process, and they were driven to solve the problem. I asked them to list the items we underlined—the things we "listened" to. One by one, we wrote the items on the board. By now they had all calmed down and were working like a crew of builders working through a problem.

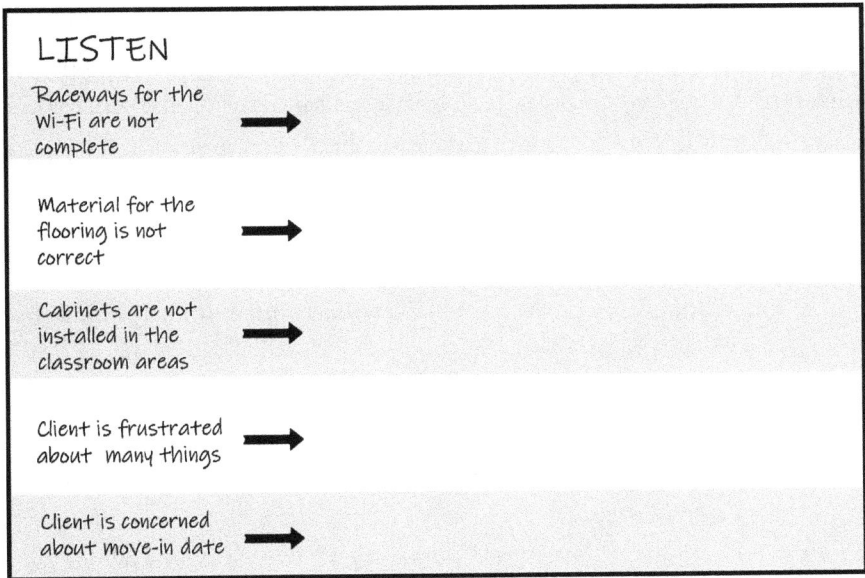

LISTEN

Raceways for the
Wi-Fi are not   ➡
complete

Material for the
flooring is not   ➡
correct

Cabinets are not
installed in the   ➡
classroom areas

Client is frustrated   ➡
about many things

Client is concerned   ➡
about move-in date

When we had the items listed, we stepped back and looked at the big picture. The team had done a great job summarizing the main points that needed to be addressed.

Plan

I said, "Now we can move to the next step in the process: Plan. We need to do some research to find answers, review the actual status of the project, take pictures, and then take action to respond and adjust actions in the field."

For each of the items listed, we drew an arrow to the right of the plan column and started working on a plan to address each of the items listed under *LISTEN*.

The information we gathered allowed the team to put a plan together based on the facts, not perceived notions. Occasionally, they would slip back to venting or try to jump ahead to the solution. Each time, I would redirect them to stick with the subject at hand. To go back to the map and road trip analogy, we were currently defining the different routes we could take. They were jumping to the final route and deciding before all the information had been assessed. The cool thing about this process is that it slows you down and makes you look at all information and how it ties together. It allows you to make the best decision with all the information you have at the time.

For the first item, Eddie said, "We need to go out and look at the area to confirm it is complete or assess what needs to be done to finish the area."

I said, "Good. Seeing the area may help clear up the misunderstanding. Either the rep has not seen it or he has seen it and is seeing something we have not."

As we moved down the items in the *LISTEN* column, Andrew said, "We need to review the specifications to see what material requirements are there."

Eddie said, "Good, that will help define the standard for the installation too. For the next item, we need to call the subcontractor to find out the status of the material delivery. It was ordered five weeks ago and should have been there by now."

"For the last two items, we need to do some research. The owner says they are frustrated about a lot of things, and they are concerned about the move-in date. I think we need some clarification from them on these two items," Andrew said.

LISTEN	PLAN	
Raceways for the Wi-Fi are not complete	➡️	Review in field for status ➡️
Material for the flooring is not correct	➡️	Check the specifications for requirements included ➡️
Cabinets are not installed in the classroom areas	➡️	Call for the status of order ➡️
Client is frustrated about many things	➡️	Requested specific list of items ➡️
Client is concerned about move-in date	➡️	Requested specific concerns ➡️

I said, "OK, you have some good information and a good plan. The next step is to do all the things in the *PLAN* column. Do your research, talk to people, and come back with the answers to solidify the plan. Then, enter the action you will take under the *BUILD* column. Then execute those actions and build a solution. You can track each of the action items to the right of the list."

I stopped before walking out of the job site office and said, "Good job, guys. The thing to watch is moving too quickly to a solution in the *BUILD* column." Analyze each item in the *LISTEN* column and create a plan for that item. It may be research, discovering an actual condition, talking to people involved, or gaining more perspective and knowledge. You are on the right path. Remember, during the entire process it will be easy to slip back into venting mode." I reminded them of the four mindsets:

1. Solve the problem.
2. Always think about what you can do.

3. Always be curious.
4. Always improve your situation.

Eddie said, "Thanks, Doug. We were too emotional, and we weren't focusing on solving the real problem. Venting stopped us from improving our situation, and we were thinking more about proving our point than thinking about what we can do. We weren't moving forward, were we?"

I said, "No . . . but you are now, and that's all that matters."

Eddie said, "We can get back on track on the project. We have this, boss. Thanks."

Build

Later that day, we met as a team.

Eddie presented all the information and wrote the solutions in the *BUILD* column before the meeting. He was prepared.

LISTEN	PLAN	BUILD
Raceways for the Wi-Fi are not complete	Review in field for status	Meet with client on findings
Material for the flooring is not correct	Check the specifications for requirements included	Meet with client on findings
Cabinets are not installed in the classroom areas	Call for the status of order	Delivery next week. Follow up
Client is frustrated about many things	Requested specific list of items	Request list. Meet with client Ask client to bring list to discuss
Client is concerned about move-in date	Requested specific concerns	Request list. Meet with client to discuss list

I said, "Each item, as you can see, has an element of having to communicate information to the client and the client's representative."

Eddie said, "Yes, we can compose an email to respond to each of them with the actual status to give them a better understanding."

I smiled and said, "Yes, that is one solution. But is it the most effective solution?"

The team looked puzzled.

"Effective?" Andrew said.

"Yes, effective. There is a lot of tension among all of us now. The information is one thing. How do we ease the tension and bring the entire team back together—the client, the rep, the architect, and our company?"

Eddie looked up from his notes and said, "We need to meet face-to-face."

"Yes," I said, "we need to sit down together and go through every-thing face-to-face. That's the best way. Set up the meeting and let's get this project back on track."

Tools for Your Toolbox

When you use the blueprint of Listen Plan Build, you will find a path to solve your challenges. You will be more effective in whatever you do. Notice I use the word *effective*, not *successful*. When you are effective, you are moving the needle; you are moving forward. You will have fail-ures and you will not always be successful in the short term. But when you are effective, you will be successful in the long term.

Not only do you have to perform each step of Listen Plan Build, but also you must do them in the right order. We've all observed folks who want to jump in and figure it out as they go. That does work. At times they get lucky, and they are successful. But over time, there will be more failures than successes. To be successful, you must build trust in those around you. To build trust you must be consistent. The method of Listen Plan Build will give you more wins than losses.

Listen, plan, and *build* are not buzzwords. They are a blueprint that will build your potential into effective leadership. Apply Listen Plan Build as a blueprint to every challenge you face.

In Chapter 6 we will explore the true meaning of those three words and give examples of how you can use them every day to lead and to learn.

While you must have the technical skills to build projects, the goal is also to have the ability to build others around you and teach others to build in the future. Please understand that you must have technical ability and heart, because when things get hard, you must have the heart to push through and believe that Listen Plan Build will get you where you need to be. The standard is high. At every turn, you must listen to understand—not to respond—and then plan without ego with the cause in mind. Only then can you build.

The Tools

1. Listen Plan Build is a process to be more effective in whatever you do.
2. You will have short-term failure and long-term success. The process allows you to adapt when things don't go as planned or you learn new information.
3. When things get hard or you get stuck, apply Listen Plan Build as a blueprint to every challenge you face.

7

LISTEN

Listening is the key to starting the process to solve challenges. **Remember, you don't know what you don't know.** Chris Voss calls it the "Black Swan" in his book *Never Split the Difference*.[3] The Black Swan is the thing you don't know about a situation. There are Black Swans in every challenging situation—things that would change the way you approach a challenging situation if you only knew about them. I want to stress to you how important listening, reading, researching, and gathering information is to the problem-solving process. You need these to become a part of your everyday life and a part of the culture of your organization.

1. There are things you know from your perspective. Your experiences drive your perspective and may influence decisions based on what you know or may not know.
2. There are things you may not understand from another person's perspective. Their experience may be completely different than yours, and their perspective could have an impact on the decisions to be made.

---

[3] Chris Voss, *Never Split the Difference: Negotiating as if Your Life Depended on It* (New York: Harper Business, 2016).

3. And sometimes you just don't know what you don't know. No one has experienced everything, and you may encounter a situation that you and your team have zero knowledge about.

All of these things are cured by one simple mindset: Be curious. Be curious to learn if your perspective may be skewing your information. Be curious to understand another person's information and perspective. Be curious to find out what you don't know.

A Listening Culture—Lifelong Learning

I was just finishing a hospital project in Modesto, California, in January 1997 when Tim called and gave me my next assignment. Our company had just been awarded a $26 million-dollar intermediate school in Clovis, California. After working in multiple towns over the last six years, it would be great to work closer to where I grew up in Fresno.

Be curious to learn, to understand, to find out what you don't know.

I was dating a wonderful girl at the time, and I asked her if she wanted to come to Fresno with me. She looked at me and said, "I don't know . . . are we getting married?"

I looked at her, puzzled, because as odd as it was, I think *she* had just proposed to *me*!

I said, "Yes!" and we started making plans for our new life together.

I started as an assistant project manager for the new Reyburn Intermediate School in April 1997, and Jodi and I were married five months later. I had no idea how important 1997 would be in my life and my career. Reyburn Intermediate was to be part of the Clovis East Education Complex, the second Education Center for the Clovis Unified School District. The first was the Buchanan Education Center, named after Dr. Floyd Buchanan, who served as superintendent from 1960 to 1991 and built the culture and the values of the district. The district's culture or "why" was to just do what was best for the kids.

As the Reyburn project kicked off, I quickly saw the CUSD culture in action. I was lucky to work with an educator, Roger Oraze, who was the assistant superintendent of facilities, and Gerry Walker, a long-time general contractor and former school board member who was the director of facilities. Each had their own perspective—one as an educator and one as a contractor. But they also had the same cause; whether it was a problem with materials, a change of order, or the schedule, they always made a decision about how to move forward on what was best for the kids.

Over the next 25 years, I continued to work with Clovis unified on numerous projects, growing from assistant project manager, project manager, project executive, and vice president to now owner of a construction firm. In that time, 10 people in various positions changed, but the values and their cause never did. I have never experienced anything like it with any other clients. While there were disagreements, for more than 25 years, I have never been in a claim or litigation with Clovis unified, and it's because of their culture. They are true builders. They seek to build consensus, relationships, and knowledge. But they also have a high standard of safety, quality, time, and cost. They hold the line when needed and see the reality that no one is perfect in design or construction.

Charging the Hill—A Different Perspective

In the mid-1990s, a new superintendent took the helm at CUSD. I had the opportunity to sit down with Don Ulrich, former associate superintendent of facilities, and ask about the culture at CUSD.

Don explained that he and many cabinet members had been with the district since they started their careers. When Doc Buchanan retired, the long-time employees held the key to the culture and successes of the past.

At that time, funding for all schools was difficult; every district was trying to find a way to cut costs. One of the changes on the table was a cost-cutting measure that affected graduation. The new superintendent had extensive experience and a take-charge leadership style to change the district for the better. He had many initiatives that he put forth for immediate impact.

While the superintendent had many positive attributes, his drive and confidence were overriding the need to listen to those around him, much like I experienced in Charging the Hill in Chapter 1. CUSD had a strong culture of listening and a tradition of putting the students and community first. While the cabinet listened to the initiatives and the new direction, they did not give up on the standards and principles that had given them success for so many years.

As an example, CUSD held an individual graduation for each high school on different nights to allow for all seven board members to attend each graduation. The superintendent suggested holding the graduations on the same day and night to cut costs. The cabinet members and the school board were adamant that the tradition stand. It was important to the community, the board, and the students. It showed that the district cared about each graduate.

It wasn't long before the district and the superintendent parted ways, and a new superintendent by the name of Walt Buster stepped into action with a different approach. In his first cabinet meeting, he showed the true leadership CUSD needed. The first thing he did was listen. He listened to both the issues and the successes. He wanted to understand the district of which he was now a part.

Sitting in that cabinet meeting, Walt could sense the resolve in his people. He took their advice and maintained the culture and traditions. But he did so with a curious eye. He wanted to see things for himself before he made a call to change it. He listed and gathered information before putting a plan together to take action. He had an open mind to not judge before he understood. He asked questions to learn, not to prove a point. This is a quality that allowed him to navigate a district of strong traditions, make some tweaks, and get out of the way.

CUSD's philosophy is ingrained in the fabric of their culture from hiring to graduations to interactions at the job site—not just for the good things but also to solve problems. When there is a problem, CUSD does not run to their corner and prepare to fight. On the contrary, they run to the problem hand in hand with their team and work to solve it together by listening to understand, then finding the most effective solution.

Carrying on the District Culture

Don implemented these strategies when he took over for Walt Byrd, his predecessor in the facilities position. Walt had been a teacher, coach, and principal before taking the facilities position. He was instrumental in leading the project team across the finish line on the largest comprehensive education center ever built in California. Don had big shoes to fill, and he was ready.

Don went to his first meeting at a job site with the architect and the general contractor. The meeting was less than collaborative, with the architect and contractor maintaining heated battles on each issue discussed.

Don asked the architect after the meeting, "Is this how all the meetings are?"

The architect responded, "No, but it does happen."

Most of the issues being discussed seemed as though they could have been resolved before the project even started. Don told me, "It was as if the architect and contractor each held a bat behind their back, hiding information until they were ready to pound each other with the information that would support their case."

He thought there must be a way for the district to understand the process. There had to be a way to bring people together as CUSD has done for years.

Don's approach was not to find out what the architects and contractors should be doing better to avoid the fight. He wanted to know what Clovis unified could do better to be a better client and serve the designer and contractors for all projects and all delivery methods. The district had been using the CM (Construction Manager) Multi Prime project delivery method for years, and it was extraordinarily successful and collaborative. But the design-bid-build delivery method for projects was still contentious.

Right then and there, Don knew something had to change. Just like Doc and Walt, he was not going to run to a corner and fight; he was going to find a way to bring the pool of architects and CMs together to ask what, as a district, they could do better to help the construction process. But these firms were all competitors—would they want to meet? Would they openly share information? It was a long shot, but Don knew bringing people together, no matter how hard, always resulted in a positive relationship and outcome.

The Big Nine

Don's first call was to a local contractor, one of the construction managers in the pool. Don pitched the idea, and the CM's response was direct: "You want to do what? There is no way you will get everyone to agree to that. We are all competitors, and you're asking us to share information that could give our competition an edge?"

Don understood. He said, "This is not about making your competition better; this is all about making CUSD better. We have a lot of things to learn, and we need your help. We have a lot of things to think through because this has never been done before, but we trust you and all of our architects and contractors."

Thirty days later, Don had managed to get every architect and construction manager to come together in the CUSD boardroom to listen to how they could help their client.

We had all seen one another at job walks for bidding potential projects, but now we were face-to-face and coming together for the common good of a client we had all worked with for many years.

Don's first question was "How can we do things better to make the project easier for you?"

Next he asked, "What are we doing well that we should keep doing?"

Clovis USD had always had a mantra of lifelong learning, and this was the ultimate example. One of the top districts for building quality facilities in the state was taking a step back and asking how they could do better even though they were already recognized as being one of the best in the state!

Then Don asked, "What are some of the things that impact the success of projects the most?"

In a pure brainstorming fashion, the responses began:

"Constructability," one person said.

Another said, "Change orders and schedule delays."

Even more responses came from the back of the room. "Delivery methods, collaboration, communication."

Don wrote them all on the whiteboard, and for the next two hours, they discussed the best practices to achieve success in many areas.

At the end of the meeting, Don said, "I want to thank everyone for being here today and taking the time to help our district get better. Your openness will have an impact for years to come. Here are some of the takeaways and actions steps we will be focusing on:

"We will bring in the maintenance staff early to review the products and details as they relate to repairs.

"We will do 'Page Turnings' with all stakeholders, teachers, maintenance department managers, coaches, and administration at the table to review the drawings together.

"The district will lead an in-person job walk with all consultants before design starts.

"The construction managers and architects will do a combined review of the documents prior to bidding for the job and finalizing the drawings to confirm what was on-site."

Trust Is Built by Listening

The ultimate gain was the respect all the architects, engineers, and contractors gained. We could all row in the same direction and solve problems—all because we had been given permission to come together. Although no one knew it yet, this simple act of bringing competitors together would change the way all of us would do business in the future. Winning projects is the lifeblood of a construction company, but we saw that we could help a client—a cause bigger than ourselves—and still get work. No one company can do all the work in the area. We saw that it is more important to work alongside our competitors to improve the overall system for our client than to compete for *all* the projects. In doing so, we saw our competitors as human beings. Over the years, we have helped one another to get better. We've called one another for advice. Now, this doesn't mean we are not fierce rivals when we compete, but we realize that making one another better helps the industry . . . and ultimately helps us. We have grown from standing side by side with our designers, clients, and competitors to build something that has improved our industry in the San Joaquin Valley.

As an example, in 2023, 10 years after the "Big Nine" started, MWC (my company) was in the bidding phase of two projects for a client: an aquatics center and multiple soccer and baseball fields. Since these were on an existing campus, we would be building close to the students' path of travel, and safety would be a key factor over the 14-month duration of the projects.

In addition, there was a fourth phase planned—a performing arts theater that had been awarded to BUSH Construction, who would be the construction manager on that project. Their project was directly across the fire lane from our projects. Access to the three projects would have to be shared.

The performing arts project consisted of a six-story performing arts center bounded by buildings on two sides, a fire lane on the third side, and a student walkway on the fourth side. It was a very tight site—similar to buildings in downtown San Francisco. There was no room for a laydown yard or staging of materials.

Our client mentioned that the project had been submitted for approval to the state and should start construction in a few months. Given the time limit, I suggested a meeting with my company and BUSH Construction so we could coordinate access and logistics for both projects. BUSH Construction is a well-known contractor in the valley and has a good reputation. They were part of the "Big Nine," so we knew each other well in both technical terms and approach from working with Clovis Unified for the last 10 years. In addition, we had competitively bid on several projects under the multiple prime delivery method where we were supervised by BUSH construction, and BUSH competitively bid on projects that were being supervised by MWC. I'm not saying that everything was collaborative from the beginning—no relationship is—but we did develop a mutual respect and admiration for each other over the years. Clovis Unified did a great job of keeping all of us focused on the project and not on our own interests.

Our client scheduled a time to meet to review the needs of all four projects. Although the client had scheduled it, they were strangely quiet as we came online for our meeting. Michael Bush, the owner of BUSH Construction, was on the call with four of his staff. As we sat there waiting, it hit me. I realized that our new client did not know about our relationship of collaboration over the years. The new client only saw that we were competitors and couldn't figure out why we would want to help each other. They had never experienced two competitors coming together for a common cause and working through the needs together for interests other than their own. Their experience was driving their perception of MWC and BUSH Construction.

So, I decided to break the ice by saying sarcastically, "Wow, Michael, you have a really tight site. Sure glad MWC isn't on that project—it's going to be tough."

The entire BUSH staff broke out in laughter as did the MWC staff. Our client smiled nervously, so I continued. "I guess we could let you have some of our site for staging and laydown if you need some help, but it's going to cost you."

Still laughing, Michael said, "That's very kind of you, Mr. Reitz."

With that, the client now understood that we had worked together a lot over the years, we trusted each other, and we were truly there to solve the problem and do what was best for the client. We all discussed options for about 45 minutes and came up with a solution that would allow the performing arts center to be built as efficiently as possible and still maintain the needs of the athletics department for the state-of-the-art baseball and softball complex. We would hold off on completing one of the practice fields so BUSH could use it for laydown, job offices, and staging. While this was not best for our project, wasn't perfect for BUSH's project, and wasn't ideal for the client because it would delay putting a practice field into use, it was what was best for all the projects combined.

This was the ultimate lesson in listening, planning, and building for improvement in all areas of the industry. The result is that the members of the Big Nine have taken these ideas and spread the philosophy to other districts, thus showing the benefit of listening to one another to be better for the common good.

Tools for Your Toolbox

The power of being a builder and using the Listen Plan Build process is that it gives you a mindset and confidence that you will be a more effective leader when you solve challenges by listening to others first. It allows you to gain information by being open to all you hear. While you as the leader must ultimately give direction to the team, you do not do so without first listening. You must listen to all parties, build on that information, and make the best decision possible for the cause.

As the leader, you must know "where you are" and "where you want to go" and define the actual problem. Listening is the first step to gaining the knowledge to make the best plan for acting (building).

Clovis unified did exactly that. They took a step outside of the standard practices and brought people together (which had never been done before) and listened so they could become stronger and more effective for the kids of their district. As a by-product, everyone in the room gained a better knowledge and respect for one another and developed relationships that had never been formed before. The knowledge and relationships are now further reaching and improving design and construction in the San Joaquin Valley.

> Know "where you are" and "where you want to go".

You must listen to understand, not to respond. You must be curious. You must have curiosity for what the other person is thinking, to learn something new, or to confirm what you already know. You must have empathy to relate to and understand what the real issue is or at least the perception of the real issue.

To listen means to gather information. It could be written or verbal. The true test of the system is to be able to listen in both easy and difficult situations. As a leader, you will be put into difficult situations when you don't agree with the person to whom you are talking.

They may even be attacking you and your knowledge. This is the most important time to listen.

When approaching a problem, think to yourself:

1. *I could be wrong.*
2. *There may be information I am missing, and it is causing a misunderstanding.*
3. *The other person is wrong, and I will be responsible for conveying a new perspective.*

Your mindset should be that of a detective. You must detach from the emotion and learn all you can. You may learn that your perspective is skewed because of limited information.

You want to get to the best solution for the situation, not for you and not for them. The more you learn, the more you will know, the better decisions you will make to move forward. It's not about being right or wrong. It's all about finding the most effective solution for the problem at hand.

The Tools

1. Listening is the first step to gaining the knowledge to make the best plan. Remember, you may learn something that will affect your perspective.
2. You must listen to understand, not to reply.
3. You must be curious to dig deeper to find the best information.
4. You must have empathy to relate to your team's perspective and understand what the real issue is for them. Only then can you truly address it and be most effective.

8

PLAN

As a leader, there are three huge hurdles in the human mind when it comes to planning with your team:

1. We have no knowledge of the situation or issue and don't want to look incompetent, so let's just dig in and see where it takes us.
2. We have done this before, so let's just do what we have always done.
3. We're not really sure what to do, so let's put the perfect plan together before we start.

You may have thought these things as well over the length of your career. Let's explore each of the scenarios and then talk about what the best approach actually is.

1. **We have no knowledge of the situation or issues and don't want to look incompetent, so let's just dig in and see where it takes us.** Many times, you probably don't want to admit to your team that you have never done something like this before. Going through the planning process would reveal your lack of knowledge to your team. You

might say something like "Let's get started on our own individual tasks and check back together next week." This is
kicking the can down the road. So, for a week no one is
coordinated, and there is no path or priority to the action.
When you get back together, not much has been accomplished, so someone asks, "I'm not sure what we are trying
to accomplish; can you go over it again, please?" Or your
boss asks, "How is the task going? Are we still on track to
complete the project on schedule?" Either way, you are in a
tough spot because you don't have a handle on the plan or
the ultimate goal.

2. **We have done this before, so let's just do what we have
always done.** The thing about life is that no matter how
many times you have done something, there are variables
that will make it different. Someone may be having a bad day,
there's a new member on the team, you encounter shipping
and delivery issues, and so forth. For example, you can take
the same route to work every day, at the same time, driving
the same speed, and there could be a 5- to 10-minute varia-
tion in the time it takes to get to work. Traffic, weather, and
days of the week all could have an impact on your journey.
You may even have to take a detour because of an accident.
Be open to the variations and plan contingencies to allow
you to accomplish your task on time.

3. **We're not really sure what to do, so let's put the perfect plan together before we start.** From there, you and
your team try to put the perfect plan together to cover every
contingency, and after two months of planning, you still
haven't taken any action toward starting or completing the
project. This relates directly to the "paralysis by analysis" we
discussed earlier. Whether you have never done something
or have done it a hundred times before, there is no physical

way to account for variables. You can plan forever to try to capture the perfect plan. But as Mike Tyson said, *"Everyone has a plan until they get hit in the face,"* or in military terms, *"No plan survives first contact."* The only consistent thing about life is that it is inconsistent.

Planning is a dichotomy: having no plan versus planning for every contingency. Neither one is effective. You must find the balance in every situation and use an iterative (step-by-step) plan like the puzzle scenario. Start with the things you know and set a process and a timeline. Then gather a list of potential issues and develop areas you could adapt to if something unexpected comes along. As a leader and a builder, it is your responsibility to lead your team through the process and build a plan that finds the balance between starting the process and having contingencies when things need to adapt.

> The only consistent thing about life is that it is inconsistent.

To plan, you must have a goal and lay all the facts on the table that you gained from gathering information in the Listen phase. The plan must focus on the overall mission—what is best for the project or goal. Lay out all the things you have gained from listening and develop a plan to address each of the items. This is not the action of resolving the issue. It is defining the plan to act. This may include research on information needed, lead times, people who may have additional information, review of the contract documents, and so forth.

Part of the plan may be to wait and see what happens. Deciding to wait is an action when further information can develop. Not all waiting is procrastination when you have a specific goal.

There are times when you must make a decision that requires you to listen for the big-picture items and put a plan in place in a matter of hours. There will be things you don't know and must make your best guess—one of the most gut-wrenching things to do. It requires you to detach from your stress and focus on a cause bigger than yourself.

Friday Night Lights

This was the case in 2008 while building a stadium in the small rural community where Jodi and I raised our kids. My first project as a project manager had been to build the high school just eight years earlier. It is a wonderful place with a great school district. We were awarded the new stadium project, and I was excited to be building a project close to home. I was proud to be involved with the project because my daughter was on the youth cheer squad, and she would get to use the stadium to cheer on the youth football teams. Youth football in high school was straight out of the movies. Parents would pull their trucks up to the track and watch the game from their tailgates. That year the team was doing very well in the conference, and the stadium would take the community to the next level. That is, until everything came unraveled.

The infrastructure for the stadium project was going well. The stadium contractor had slipped on the schedule, but we were still OK. Over the next few weeks, we heard less and less from the stadium contractor . . . and finally nothing but crickets. I called Tim to go over my concerns.

"Tim," I said, "I have been calling the stadium contractor for the last three days and still have no answer. I haven't been able to get any updates on material or fabrication; everyone is being elusive."

Fearing the worst, he said, "Get on a plane to Texas tonight. We must find out what is going on."

Not six months earlier we had been on the phone after receiving a bid verifying scope, schedule, and numbers. They were quite a bit lower on their bid than the others, but they said they had everything covered, including the fact that they had a new plant and were ready to show the country how they use their state-of-the-art equipment to be less expensive and more efficient.

We had done several of these types of projects, and all seemed to be legit.

I flew out of Fresno to Dallas, Texas, rented a car, and drove three hours to Graham, Texas.

It was hot and humid; I wasn't in California anymore. I passed the hotel and drove straight to the stadium manufacturers' office. As I went in, it was strangely quiet. I asked to speak to the owner, and a nice person shuffled me to his office.

As I entered the office, he had his head down reviewing paperwork. As he looked up, I saw a completely disheveled and stressed man. I introduced myself, and an "oh my God" look came over his face. He asked, "What brings you out to Texas?"

I said, "Well, we haven't had a lot of communication over the last few weeks. We'd like to see things firsthand to see how we can help."

He sat there quietly staring at his hands.

Realizing there must be some heavy issues on his mind, I sat down and said, "I came to listen to what is going on and see if we can help in any way. After we talk, I would like to get together with you to put a plan together to get this project across the finish line."

We talked for a while. He seemed to be avoiding the actual status of our project. I said, "I'm sure with the new facility and all the work you have, there must be some delays in fabrication, right? Tell me about the situation, and we will see how we can rearrange the schedule to help everyone."

After some hemming and hawing, he broke down and said, "I am filing for bankruptcy."

My heart sank. I had never experienced a subcontractor failure before. Sure, there were people on the verge of failing, but we had always been able to shore them up and get the project finished. There was no way we could survive this and meet the needs of the school. We had never failed before, and this project was about to be the first.

I told the owner of the company that I needed to make a few calls and would be right back. I looked him straight in the eye and said confidently, "We will get through this."

I immediately picked up the phone and gave Tim a call to download all the information. At the end of the call, Tim made two statements.

"Doug, you are there, and you have the best perspective to make the call on the best plan based on what you see. You've got this."

I said, "Thanks for the confidence, Tim. I have never handled anything like this before."

He said, "Doug, this is difficult, but you're a builder. Take things step-by-step and build the most effective solution possible."

There's a quote I had read many years earlier from Colonel Hal Moore: "There is *always* one more thing you can do."

After I got off the phone, I sat down in their conference room and started writing questions. I listened and gathered as much information as possible very quickly. I wrote these questions:

1. Is the steel in the yard and how much has been fabricated?
2. Where is the press box?
3. Who do they have to install the stadium?
4. Do they have the aluminum for the bleachers?
5. Do they have someone to ship the materials to California?

I went back to the owner, and he introduced me to his operations person, Frank Beaman. I asked him each of the questions to get a 60,000-foot view of the situation. I learned these facts:

1. We have steel in the yard.
2. The press box was fabricated by someone else three hours from Graham.

3. Installation is by a contractor in California.
4. The aluminum had not been purchased, but he gave me their contact details.

Frank said, "There is one more problem. From rumors in town, the sheriff plans to lock the gates by noon tomorrow."

I said, "That doesn't matter; we have already paid for the steel you have in the yard; it's ours."

He said, "Yes, but that will have to be determined by all the receipts and a judge. It will take months to sort out."

"There must be another way," I said. "Can we get a trucking company to move it out today?"

"No one will work for us because we are so far in debt. You are welcome to go tag the steel that's yours, but you will need a hat—it's hot out there—and watch out for the rattlesnakes; they like to shade themselves under the steel in the afternoon."

The Plan

As I walked out, I saw that the facility was state of the art, and the gravel lot was surrounded by thick scrub brush with the sound of rattlesnakes' rattles singing across the yard.

I began the arduous task of comparing the shop drawings to the marks on the steel. While I was tagging steel from the list, I looked up to see a tall, thin, very tan man with a beard.

He said, "My name is Dan; I heard you are from California."

I smiled and said, "Yeah, this is quite the predicament we are in."

He agreed. He told me this was his last day. "This is a small town, and I need to start looking for another job," he said. "Frank had told me about the project and what you are trying to do. I have a friend in town with a truck, and he can get the steel out this afternoon."

I said, "That would be great, but I don't know how to drive a fork-lift, and I'm not sure where to store it."

Dan said, "No problem; I can help you out. I'll give him a call while you finish tagging the steel."

After about an hour and a half in the sweltering heat, I finished tagging all the steel I could.

Dan came back and said, "My buddy will be here about 5:00 p.m. He has a plot of land where we can store the steel as long as we need to."

I said, "Thank you." But in the back of my mind, I couldn't help but think there was a catch. I was heading back home in a couple of days. They could easily sell the steel to someone else; there was no way to know if they were truly helping or if they had an ulterior motive.

Nonetheless, Dan started sorting the steel into an area to allow the truck to have access, and while I knew hope was not a plan, it was all I had now.

About 5:00 p.m. the truck showed up on schedule, and Dan loaded him up. It took three trips to get the steel out. While they loaded the steel, I found an ATM and pulled out cash to pay the trucker and Dan. They both said they didn't want anything, but I had to do something for them. They both stepped up to help me out and had no reason to do it other than they were good people and saw that they could help.

I got back to the hotel and called Jodi. I told her the whole story.

She said, "It sounds like you were able to build trust with the guys, and they are willing to help."

I said, "It sure seems that way." I told her I would be there for a couple more days to get things sorted out.

My next call was to the airline to move my flight and then extend my hotel.

The next morning, I drove back to the fabrication plant. As I drove up the tree-lined road, I saw that the gates were closed, and a sign on the gate said "CLOSED BY ORDER OF THE SHERIFF" in big red letters.

It was padlocked, and the place was empty.

I sat there for a moment with great relief. The actions we had taken the previous afternoon and evening saved the project. Had we not moved quickly, the project would have been delayed for months while everything got sorted out. My gratitude to Dan and the trucker was immense.

As I was sitting there thinking, my phone rang. It was a Texas area code.

I said, "This is Doug."

The voice on the other end said, "Doug, this is Frank Beaman. I want to let you know the sheriff locked the doors at 8:00 p.m. yesterday. Were you able to get the steel out?"

I said, "Yes, we did; we finished at 7:00 p.m."

"Good to hear," he said. "Doug, I made some calls to some of our partners in the industry, and I think I have a plan for you. Can you come by my house this morning so we can go through it?"

I said, "Send me the address, and I'll head over right now."

As I walked up to the house, Frank met me at the door with a smile. I said, "Frank, I can't thank you enough for helping us out."

He said, "No problem. I'm impressed with the way you and your company have handled this whole situation. You didn't lawyer up; you just wanted to find a solution. That doesn't happen very often in these situations. Let's go back to my office and lay out a plan."

As we sat down, he pulled out a sheet of paper with a list of companies and phone numbers. Frank had been in the industry for years and had a lot of contacts.

He explained that he had made some calls yesterday, and while it was not ideal, he had found a place to fabricate the bleacher steel in Virginia, secured a place to get the aluminum parts for the bleachers' seating and siding, and contacted a place a few hours away to fabricate the press box. Lastly, he gave me the name and number of an installer in California who specialized in installing bleachers.

It was nothing short of amazing.

We proceeded to call each of the companies, set up trucking, and create a timeline for all the work. After a few hours, everything was arranged.

The timeline was behind what we had hoped for but well ahead of where we would be if we didn't have the steel.

Before I left, I asked Frank how we could compensate him for his time. He said, "Doug, my compensation is helping you and seeing that the project gets done."

I thanked him, and with that, I headed back to the hotel to report to everyone about the plan.

To this day, I still don't know why all the great people I met in Graham, Texas, jumped in and trusted us so quickly and truly did whatever it took to help.

I will never forget them and their generosity.

The stadium was completed per plan and on a revised schedule. We phased the project to give the high school access to games, and we worked around all the athletic needs. The leadership at the school district never ran to their own corner; they were right there helping to solve the problem with the rest of the team. This would not have occurred without the help of Frank Beaman, Dan, the trucking company, the fabrication companies across the country, the athletic director, the principal district staff, and the school board members. One final thank-you goes to Mike and Cody Russell who worked overtime to build the stadium. They took complete ownership of making sure everything went according to plan during construction.

Tools for Your Toolbox

The key to the success of the stadium project was that the plan was developed by multiple members on the team, and they had buy-in for the goal they were trying to achieve. As a leader and a builder, always develop the plan with your team. They will not only have critical background knowledge as they implement the plan, but they will also have buy-in when things get tough that will allow them to push through. It will not lessen the respect your team has for you by being open and asking questions. On the contrary, it will serve to elevate their respect for you because you value their opinion, whether it is ultimately included in the plan or not.

A good plan serves two purposes. One, it gives you something to target or shoot for when you are dealing with the heavy details and tasks. Two, it gives you a measuring stick to see how you are progressing. Remember, it is an iterative process. You must approach it in increments. It is similar to the process fighter pilots use in a dogfight called the OODA Loop Theory.

The process was defined by John Boyd, an air force pilot, and the military created the OODA Loop Theory for pilots to make decisions:

- Observe
- Orient
- Decide
- Act

Pilots in air-to-air combat learned that if they reacted to the current situation and stayed the course, they would probably lose the dogfight. Instead, they had to continually observe the situation, look for changes, reorient, make the call, and implement the action—over and over and over. These were the pilots that had the greatest success.

Planning is a continuous process even as you begin to take action.

As a builder, you must realize that the plan you and your team come up with is a tool to achieve the end goal of what you are trying to build. There will be successes and setbacks. You must adapt, reorient your plan, and always keep building.

The Tools

The challenges we had with the stadium project are like most challenges you will encounter:

1.   There will always be unknowns in every situation.
2.   At times it will seem impossible.
3.   Look to those around you to help with the plan.

Don't be frustrated when things don't go perfectly according to plan. The plan will continue to evolve, and that's OK as long as you continue to move forward. Stay positive and help your team adapt and carry on.

9

BUILD

The beauty of living in the San Joaquin Valley in California is not only the diversity of people and cultures, but also the quick access to the arts and culture in the Bay area, the beaches of the Central Coast, and the breathtaking views of the Sierra Mountains. Growing up so close to Yosemite, my mom and dad took us there often. As my wife and I started our family, we continued the tradition; Jodi and I even had our honeymoon in Yosemite Valley. We would hike Vernal Falls, Yosemite Falls, and the entire valley floor, looking up at El Capitan and seeing the rock climbers perilously making their way to the top of the 3,000-foot granite face. But there is one thing that had loomed in my mind for years.

As you come out of the tunnel on Highway 120, the first thing that comes into view is a look down at the valley that is anchored at the end by Half Dome. From the valley floor, it is an 18-mile hike with an elevation gain from the valley floor of nearly 5,000 feet.

Climbing to the top of Half Dome was a bucket-list item of mine, but there was no way I could even consider it given my physical condition. With all the stress of work, I had ballooned to 250 pounds and had high blood pressure. My eating habits were poor at best, and I knew I needed to make a change.

Over the next few years, I started running, ate better, and lost weight. It was an arduous process. I started by walking, then tried to run a ¼ mile, then a ½ mile, then ¾ of a mile, and finally a full mile. The weight was coming off, and I was feeling better, and I maintained running a few miles a few times a week. I had built a new habit.

In 2017, my friend Rachel asked me to come out to a running club she belonged to. Rachel worked with her dad and family at a local architecture firm we had done business with for years. I declined multiple times because I didn't have the confidence that I could keep up with the group. Finally, about a year later, I decided to accept her invitation, and I joined the running club. The men in charge of the group were Coach Ray and his longtime friend Coach Rich. As I came out week after week, I began to meet more people. Coach Ray made me feel at home with his lighthearted jabs and encouragement. The group was amazing; it catered to all levels of walking and running, and Coach Ray kept us all together with challenges and loops. We ran at Woodward Park, the home of the State Championship Cross Country Meet. It is challenging, with long trails and killer hills. Over time, we invited people from the company and other firms to run, talk, and feel better about ourselves and our health. One of my longtime friends, Aya, started coming out as well. She is a partner in another architecture firm in Fresno. We would all talk business, leadership, and construction while we ran.

Over the next few years, we all entered many local 5K and 10K races, and my kids even started running with us as they entered cross country in middle and high school. Rachel and I decided to enter the Two Cities half marathon in November 2019. We trained a few times a week and felt good about race day. The race started off well, with a 9-minute pace. We ran from Fresno to Clovis and back. We were not the fastest, but we were steady. Now, I had heard about hitting the wall and the runner's high. I had experienced the runner's high but not the wall. That is, until mile 12. As we were in the final stretch, my legs looked up at my brain and said, "We are done." No matter how much I willed myself to run, I could not make it happen. Rachel and I walked for a bit, and I tried to run, but it wasn't getting better. After about half a mile and a bit of water, we ran the last half mile and finished the race.

That day taught me some great lessons.

- Training is important, and it takes time to build up endurance.
- Starting something new is awkward and maybe even embarrassing, but it's necessary to grow and be more effective.
- Muscles versus brain—your brain can hinder your progress. Your body has much more to offer than your brain will let you know.

Half Dome

In February 2020, Aya called and asked if we should try for the lottery to get a slot to hike Half Dome. I said, "Yes! I have always wanted to hike Half Dome!" This would give me a new challenge to focus on.

Through sports and music, I had been challenged physically, but never to this level. As it turns out, the half marathon lesson of how far I could push myself would play a large role in our hike to Half Dome.

This was an ultimate test of the builder philosophy. This is a hike that could take 10 to 12 hours.

In May 2020, we got the notification that our group had been selected for a slot in October 2020. We started training immediately—running during the week and hiking the San Joaquin River Trail just north of Millerton Lake in Madera County on the weekends. The main attraction there is Pincushion Peak: 1,200 feet of elevation gain in 1.4 miles. There are two trails, one meandering around the mountain and one heading almost straight up the mountainside. We started with Pincushion, doing three miles on the weekend, and slowly worked our way up to the 15-mile mark following along the San Joaquin River. But it still wasn't close to our 18 miles and 5,000 feet of elevation.

The group decided to take a preliminary hike to Pear Lake in Sequoia National Park. Robert, one of Aya's partners in the architecture firm, led the group, coaching us on the right things to bring in case of an emergency, being prepared for staying the night if someone was hurt, bringing plenty of food and water, and navigating the trails. Hiking was his passion as well as leading his son's Boy Scout troop. The outdoors is where he thrived.

It was 12.8 miles with 2,400 feet of elevation gain—a beautiful, strenuous hike that took us through the bright blue sky, granite mountains, and three crystal-clear lakes. The trip took us about eight hours with a break for lunch at Pear Lake. We felt very prepared.

The day to hike Half Dome arrived, and Aya and I left Fresno at 4:00 a.m. to be ready to leave the trail head at 6:00 a.m. Everyone gathered at the parking lot, went through the plan one last time, and then headed out. We stayed together and reached the first milestone of the hike on schedule at Nevada Falls. We rested, had a snack, and headed out for the next leg.

We were all feeling good. We made it through the "meadow section" and began what would be a continuous ascent for the next five miles. As we continued without any breaks on flat land, I noticed my heart rate was elevated. Normally this wasn't a concern, but it was not lowering when I walked slower. Even resting, it would slow a bit but would spike again as soon as I started moving. A group of us took it slower until we reached the base of the "granite steps" where a ranger was checking passes.

We headed up the steps and made it to the base of Half Dome. I rested, had a snack and some water, but I still wasn't feeling well at all. There I was standing at the base of one of my bucket-list goals, and I was faced with a decision. I walked to the base and looked up at the cables, and my heart rate spiked again. I couldn't figure out what was wrong—although after returning from the hike, I realized I had not ingested the carbohydrates I should have and that in combination with the altitude, put my body into panic mode. I decided not to make the ascent and rested with some of the team. I had lunch, water, and electrolytes and waited for everyone to come down. As I sat there looking up, I reminded myself that everything happens for a reason and I could learn something from this failure.

As we started back down, I started feeling better. Aya and I were leading the way down the hill. We were a little bit behind schedule but should still make it down before dark. The trip had taken its toll on some of the group, and we spread out quite a way on the trail as we approached Nevada Falls.

The sun was setting, and the smoke from the California wildfires cast a distinct haze in the sky that made for a beautiful sunset. We were only 2 hours away from hitting the valley floor. It had been a great day despite the challenges and failures.

As the last of the group came into Nevada Falls, we noticed that one member of our group wasn't back yet. Someone said he had stopped at the bathroom. Most of the group started down the hill, and Aya and I stayed back to wait for him.

He appeared in the distance, turned the corner, and walked down into the granite clearing. Aya and I turned to see that he was pale. He stopped, looked down, and immediately began to throw up a huge amount of water. We ran over to him, helped him sit down, and asked what was wrong.

He said, "My sugar is low. I used all my sugar pills already, and the combination of insulin and the enormous exertion has dropped my blood sugar really low."

I had forgotten that he mentioned his diabetes before we left the valley floor at 6:00 a.m. He had been in the lead all day and not three hours earlier had reached the summit of Half Dome. He said he started feeling bad at the top but had eaten his last sandwich and felt better before coming down. Thinking back, he had been drifting further behind the closer we got to the valley floor of the first leg.

It was now 12-½ hours later, 6:30 p.m., and the sun was going down. We still had two hours of hiking to get down from Nevada Falls.

The problem was that he couldn't keep anything down. Food, water, nothing. We needed more information on how to handle the situation. We were extremely lucky to have cell reception from our location at Nevada Falls. We decided to call Search and Rescue for advice as well as my wife Jodi, who had been diabetic for the last 12 years.

Having seen Jodi go through ups and downs over a 12-year period, I knew how serious this could be given the location, the timing, and the sunset. So, I called Jodi and described the situation. She immediately responded that he should keep drinking and eating small amounts of food and water. It would help the sugar levels, and even if he were to throw up, something would get into his system. While I was on the phone with Jodi, Aya called Search and Rescue for advice and possible solutions. They reassured us that we should try to get off the mountain slowly, stopping to rest, taking sips of water, slowly gaining his sugar back.

We were all tired. The rest of the group headed down the last leg of the hike to the valley floor. Aya and I stayed to talk through the situation. A couple of people passing by offered up some food to help.

We sat for about 45 minutes and weighed the information we had from him, Search and Rescue, and Jodi. We asked a lot of "what ifs" as well. Here were the facts as we saw them:

1. His sugar was low but was most likely manageable, and we needed to get to the valley floor. We had food, water, and shelter. Now we needed to come up with a plan to address the best and worst cases. This was a little more difficult given the variables.

2. What if we camped at Nevada Falls for the night and hiked down in the morning? We had all the things we needed to make a small shelter and a fire, and we still had water and some food.
3. What if we walked out tonight in the dark? Would his sugar stabilize?
4. If it didn't stabilize, how would we get help in the dark on a trail with no cell service?

Neither of us had been in this situation before, but we stayed calm and analyzed the problem.

First, we were determined to know "where we are": the trail at Nevada Falls at 5:00 p.m. with darkness by 6:00 p.m. and two hours to get to the valley floor at top speed.

Second, we asked, "Where do we want to be?" The valley floor.

We weighed up all the information and decided: Hike down the mountain with two options if we had to adapt.

Plan A

1. We made the decision to stay positive and light all the way down, no matter how tired we were. We decided to break every 30 minutes to assess his sugar levels.
2. We decided to get him to talk about his family and life.
3. We had lights. We knew the trail during the day but not necessarily at night. So, we would take extra care to confirm our direction at each fork in the trail.

Plan B

1. If he got worse on the trail, one of us would head down and bring back Search and Rescue.

As I stood there at Nevada Falls, thinking about the plan and wondering how it was going to go getting down the mountain, I thought back to something my son, Nolan, had taught me.

In 2018, Nolan dedicated himself to serving our country in the Army. One Christmas he was home, and we were sharing stories around the dinner table. Nolan is one hell of a storyteller and had the whole family laughing and on the edge of their seats. At one point I asked how he and his platoon stepped into danger so easily.

Nolan said, "Dad, stand up. We don't step easily into any dangerous situation. We must support one another."

He stood up from the table and moved me to the doorway of our dining room as the whole family watched.

He said, "OK, Dad, I'm going to show you how we breach a door." He lined up behind me and grabbed the back of my collar. I was going to be the first person through the door.

> No matter how much we train, we must have a system in place for when hesitation creeps into our minds.

He continued, "When I say *boom*, that's the breach exploding, and you have to move through the door and clear the room."

I said, "OK."

"*BOOM*," he said. As I started to take a step, I felt him pushing me through the door with the hand holding my collar. With our fingers drawn like guns, just as we both did when we were kids, we entered the room. The whole family loved it.

He asked, "Did you feel me pushing on your collar?"

I said, "Yes, I did!"

He said, "No matter how much we train, we must have a system in place for when hesitation creeps into our minds; that's why we hold the collar and push. Once we take the first step into the room and see the unknown, our training kicks in and we clear the room effectively."

That's when it hit me: Jodi, as well as Search and Rescue, had taken the role of grabbing us by the collar and pushing us through the door.

As we made our way to the valley floor, Aya suggested that our fellow hiker should go at his pace. She would be second to navigate, and I would follow, taking his backpack and mine. I thought that fate is a funny thing. Not six hours earlier, I had decided not to take the cables and summit. At the time, any activity made my heart race. I hadn't eaten enough to keep my body going. I was weak and decided to take the time to eat and rest. I was devastated that I wouldn't make the final climb to meet my bucket-list goal. However, had I not stopped, I would not have had the energy or the clarity to work through the issue with Aya and ultimately to carry my pack as well as his to the valley floor.

We stuck to the plan and moved slowly down the mountain. It was an amazing thing to watch him push through a very tough situation. We watched as he became more confident and focused as his sugar stabilized. After multiple stops, we made it to the valley floor three hours later. We all congratulated and thanked one another. It was a story we will never forget, and it built relationships that are timeless.

Tools for Your Toolbox

Build is the hardest of the three principles because you must take a step into uncertainty. It's when you act that all the flaws in your plan will become strikingly evident or your plan will be confirmed to be correct. The second hardest principle? To realize there are flaws in your plan and the need to make corrections. Pushing through a "proven bad idea" because of ego can be detrimental to you, your team, and the project.

When you get to the Build phase of the challenge, you could experience a feeling of hesitation. Even though you have done your best to vet all the possibilities, there is still uncertainty about what could happen or the possibility of finding out something you didn't expect. Avoid getting paralysis by analysis; there is no perfect plan.

In the Half Dome story, there was no surefire option. Both options had drawbacks. We had taken in all the information and had come up with two plans. But the plan alone would not get us down the mountain, and we had to decide and then act. Since both options could have major consequences, we had to choose the "least bad" option and take the first step.

You must reevaluate any new information that has come to light. Implement your solution incrementally, constantly looking at the new information, revising the plan, and taking action. The Listen Plan Build tool should be used as a loop. As you take action, continue listening and planning repeatedly as new information comes to light. You won't avoid setbacks and failures, but because you are moving forward incrementally, the failures and setbacks will be smaller and easier to overcome. That will lead to a smoother path to success.

The Tools

1. Avoid getting paralysis by analysis. Take small, incremental steps to move toward your goal.
2. You must take a step into uncertainty. The first step is always the hardest. Take the step!
3. Reevaluate any new information that has come to light. Don't be afraid to modify what you are doing. Just keep building!

Part III

BEING A BUILDER

10

BUILDING YOURSELF

In the construction industry, there is something we call *scope creep*. During the design process, the clients tell the architect what they would like included in the project. The concept design is completed, and an estimate of costs is performed. This estimate confirms the costs for the project, and it is compared to the client's budget for the project. During design, the project passes through schematic, design development, and construction document phases. At each phase, there is a review by the client, and a new estimate is performed. This is done to confirm the project is still on track for the client's budget. By performing estimates or an analysis at each phase of design, you build confidence that you are going to meet the goal. If you do not stop to analyze, however, you can be affected by the changes on bid day and find you are not even close to where you thought you would be on budget, causing a lot of stress and conflict.

Through these phases, the client often adds or changes scope. None of the changes in themselves are impactful to the budget; however, taken over time, all of them can wildly change the cost of the project.

When the project finally bids and the costs come in, there can be huge surprises that leave the whole team wondering, "How did we get here and how did we get so far over budget?"

This is like what you do in your career. As you progress and learn your job, get promoted, learn more, get promoted again, and continue to grow, sometimes you end up someplace you never thought you would be. Sometimes it's good, sometimes it's not, and sometimes it ends up with a huge surprise.

You Are Making the Biggest Mistake of Your Life

It was late 2013 and Tim Marsh, my boss, mentor and friend had announced his retirement. His philosophy had single-handedly taken the company from the brink of bankruptcy to being the premiere builder in the San Joaquin Valley everyone wanted to work for and work with. Architects, clients, subcontractors, and staff were lining up to be a part of what Tim Marsh had built.

In the 1990s, almost all public works projects ended in claims or litigation. Tim's mission was to change that by simply doing what a builder would do. He was focused on the challenge and the mission and not personal gain. As the title of Bill Walsh's book *The Score Will Take Care of Itself* means, when you follow the process and stay disciplined and diligent, growth and money will come as a result.

I was lucky to have been able to work with Tim for more than 23 years. I had never worked anywhere else. He mentored me through work and life, constantly encouraging me to focus on "doing the right thing" for the long term in both my family and my professional career.

On December 2, 2013, the owner of the company asked me to go to lunch, and I thought, *This is it. He is going to announce me as the next president of the company.*

I knew more about the culture of the employees, the clients, and the designers we worked with than anyone at the company. I had been involved in the field, office, financials, and bonding. I knew I could do this.

Over the last five years, he had endorsed my promotion to vice president, made me a partner in the company, and supplied unprecedented bonuses for the work that I had done. We even had a brochure depicting and introducing the management team going into the future.

As we sat down, he made some small talk and then cut to the chase.

He said, "Doug, you are not qualified to run the company. We have hired a recruiter who is doing a search over the western states for the new president."

I sat there stunned as the owner of the company told me this, after nearly 24 years with all the discussions and preparation. The rest of the world went away. I could barely hear what he was saying. In my mind, he was cold and unfeeling like it was just another business transaction.

He said, "You have only seen one company and only known one way of doing business. The next president needs to be from a larger company that will help us double in volume and move to projects throughout the state of California."

I did the best I could to say I understood. We ate lunch, and at the end of the lunch, I mustered up the courage to ask if I could apply for the position and go through the process.

He said, "Yes, of course."

For the next 30 days, I worked on my resume, gathering letters of reference from superintendents of schools, educators, and even the current mayor of Fresno. These were people with whom I had worked directly in personal and business situations, solving problems on a project level. They were relationships of trust that had been built over many years. Everyone supported me in any way they could.

A month later, I met with the recruiter. He had a myriad of tests and questions related to the company, many of which I couldn't see how they related to the position. We were a contractor who stayed within the San Joaquin Valley. Relationships and doing the right thing were the mainstay of our culture. I did my best, took all the tests, and answered all the questions. The recruiter scheduled an interview for the face-to-face portion of the process. It was a Saturday afternoon, and I was confident that I could convey all my strengths to show that I was ready for the position. Over the next two hours, we discussed people, management styles, and the knowledge of running a business. Then I took a long test that covered every aspect of the company. Walking out of the interview, I had a strange feeling. He hadn't been engaging, and it almost felt like he was going through the motions. He said it would be a couple of weeks before he would have all the interviews done and the data compiled.

I continued to dig in and perform my job as vice president, working through preconstruction on many projects and visiting jobs to be sure they were on track as I had done for so many years.

Then came the email with the report attached and a request to give the recruiter a call.

I called him to debrief on what he had found, and we reviewed the report. It was a detailed report on every aspect of the questions and what they meant. It was like nothing I had ever seen. Based on the interview and multiple written questions and answers, he had calculated in numbers my qualifications. He reviewed the analysis page by page and noted how lacking I was, in his opinion, in so many areas.

"The data doesn't lie," he said. "You are not qualified to run a company."

I was completely at a loss. I had been promoted, made a partner, and yet I wasn't qualified? I called Tim, spoke to my friends, and tried to make sense of what I just had been told. How did I not see this coming?

Once the search was done, to the owner's credit, he called me into his office and offered me a glass of wine (which I politely declined). He told me that the recruiter verified his thoughts. I was not qualified to run a company. He then added that I "was never even considered as a candidate." I thought, *How could a man I had worked for 23 years play games with my mind and career? Why did he let me go through the process?*

I thanked him and walked slowly out of his office.

The owner of the company held true to his word and selected a man who had years of experience running multiple larger companies. He said we were not going to change our culture, only enhance it— build on what we had to make us better. While I was completely in shock, I trusted that he knew best. He had been doing this for years, and I had an ego check that I was obviously not close to as good as I thought I was. It was hard to hear and make sense of.

Learning to Build Yourself

I did a lot of soul-searching. For the last five years, everything had led to me taking over the company. But now, it had all changed. I asked myself multiple questions.

- "Should I stay and learn?"
- "Would anyone else hire me?"
- "Do they really respect my skills?"
- "Do I make a difference in the company?"

After a lot of discussion with friends, colleagues, my parents, my wife, Jodi, and Tim, I decided to put my ego aside, stick with it, and learn everything I could to help the company go to the next level. As I had done all my career, I resolved that I would take one year to learn, grow, and search deep to see if this was the right path for me. After all, I didn't know what I didn't know yet.

Swallowing my pride, I went into the owner's office. "I am 100% in support of your decision, and I want to take this opportunity to learn and grow. I will reevaluate after one year and then decide where my career will take me."

"Reevaluate?" he said. "Doug, this is going to be a great time in your career. You will learn a lot from our new president. Give it some time; you will see."

From that day forward, I dedicated myself to the ideals of "being a builder" that my mentor, Tim Marsh, professionally had driven into my head for 23 years.

During that year, I jumped in with both feet and did everything I could to reassure my team and my new boss that we were going to learn and grow together. I put on blinders and went to work. I learned a lot about how bigger companies looked at office overhead, coding costs to projects, and setting up a structure for the future. The shift meant more time in the office for me and less time with clients and reviewing projects in the field. I was constantly being told that I had to approach things differently—that we were getting bigger, and we needed to focus on different things. The new president let me know very clearly that I did not need to see the projects; I just needed to review the data, and that would tell me everything I needed to know.

While this went against everything Tim had taught me, I did my best to follow the new philosophy.

Without knowing it, my confidence had spiraled.

I didn't know what to believe anymore.

How could I have been wrong for so many years?

At every turn I heard, "We are not doing it that way anymore." There were things I believed were not right for me, but I pushed forward. Jodi approached me several times and said, "You are miserable—why are you still working there?"

I would say, "I made the commitment. I need to stay for my team. I had hired almost everyone there over the last 15 years—how could I leave them?"

About 10 months into my one-year commitment, Jodi suggested that I talk to other businesses to gain some perspective. I scheduled an appointment with Martin Sizemore from Rudolph and Sletten and Mark Wilson, a local contractor in town. I had known R&S from my days in the Construction Employers Association. Mark had a great reputation for being a small family company in town, but I had only met him a couple of times. The meetings were very enlightening—a billion-dollar company and a 15-million-dollar company that were at two ends of the spectrum. Both men were genuine, honest, and shared the philosophies of their companies. They had a huge impact on me.

During the meeting with Mark, he asked, "Are you looking to leave?"

I said, "No, I know this will work out, and I just needed to get things straight in my head."

But the conversation kept playing in my head. Even the billion-dollar company reinforced the notion of it being a family organization where culture, clients, and people came first. They were builders.

The Awakening

The following week, my company held its 100-year anniversary celebration event. During the celebration, I was sitting with the other vice president, Robert Willis, as the owner gave his speech. Robert had come up through the trades. His ability to build technical expertise as well as build relationships with clients was one of the reasons the company was so successful. We were a perfect team—he with the technical ability and me with the college experience. My respect for him carries on to this day.

The event was very well attended by subcontractors and city and state dignitaries. After a lot of company history and recognizing various dignitaries, the owner said, "Ladies and gentlemen, I would like to introduce to you the future of our company who will take this company to the next level, our new president."

The new president rose and moved to the microphone where he gave a speech.

Robert and I sat there in disbelief. There it was, laid out for the hundreds in attendance—employees, dignitaries, subcontractors, clients, and designers. Robert and I, after 23 years with the company, were not a part of the plan for the future of the company.

As I went home and described the event to Jodi, I was eerily calm. I saw it clearly for the first time. I was the one the company could count on to do the heavy lifting but not someone who was vital to the future of the company. I asked Jodi, "What should I do now?"

My usually loving and compassionate wife moved from support to direct advice. "Shit or get off the pot!"

The next day I picked up the phone and called Mark Wilson. I asked if he had time to meet. We scheduled a meeting for the following week. I described the situation over the last year, and he described his situation. A couple of months earlier, a key employee left the company to move out of state for his family. Mark was planning to retire, and this employee was part of the transition. We laughed about the timing and how the planets align every so often.

Mark asked if I would want to take over the company someday.

I said, "Yes, that would be a great thing, but I think I have a lot to learn."

He said, "Well, I believe you can do that, but I would like to start slow." His plan was to transition over time; nothing was for sure or in writing. His only rule was that I would come on board as a project manager. He wanted me to work with every field team in the company before taking over. He wanted me to get to know the people and the culture. He said he would get me an offer letter with all the terms and conditions. I thanked him and said I would talk to Jodi and get back to him after the weekend.

He sent me an offer letter that by all intents and purposes was a step backward for my career. I went through the offer with Jodi. It was a demotion from vice president to project manager, with a 30% cut in pay in a company that performed 10% of the current volume I was used to. But it was a family organization that had the potential to go back to what I believed in. Without hesitation, Jodi said, "We will make it work." I was shocked, but it was a huge weight off my shoulders.

On Monday I called Mark and accepted the offer. To this day, he does not know this, but before he ended the call, he announced to his office, "Ladies and gentlemen, we got Doug Reitz," and I heard nothing but cheers over the phone as he then hung up. I sat in my car and tears filled my eyes. I was in awe—someone believed that I could bring value to them. I had sunk so low in my mind that I didn't believe I could bring value to anyone; my confidence was at an all-time low. It was a defining moment in my career that I needed to believe in the philosophy of being a builder, that all people offer value, and that you just need to be, as Jim Collins, author of the book *Good to Great*, says, "in the right seat on the right bus."

That night I drafted my letter of resignation. As I got back to work that day, I was immersed in emotions I could not separate. *How could I leave my friends and colleagues? But how could I stay in this situation?*

At that point I remembered an experience on the flight to Dallas to resolve the stadium issue. The flight attendant said something that for some reason came flooding back. "If we lose cabin pressure, a mask will drop in front of you. Pull it tight and put your mask on first, then assist a loved one." That was it. I had become so concerned about everyone else, I had forgotten to take care of myself first.

I had become so immersed in the day-to-day operations that I had forgotten to be true to what I believed in and lived by as I had been taught for so many years by my parents and Tim Marsh.

I walked into the president's office and gave him my letter of resignation. He was shocked, and I was so nervous I could hardly speak. The owner was out of town, and I asked the president to let him know about my decision. Later that night the owner called and asked if we could meet in a couple of days when he got back.

When he returned, we met, and he asked why I was leaving. I described in detail all the things that had occurred over the past year and that "corporate" was not a good model for me. He left my office only to come back a couple of days later. He said, "Doug, I have an offer for you. If you don't want to do corporate, I will set up a company for you and we will be 50/50 partners and you can keep it small and family-oriented. We want you to stay."

I thanked him and politely declined for the last time.

He stood up, looked down at me, pointed his finger, and said, "You are making the biggest mistake of your life."

I looked back, and with a slight smile, I said, "That may be so, sir, but I need to follow what I believe."

Thanks to my wife, my parents, my friends, and my coworkers, I began to believe in being a builder again. Mark's methodical approach to building the transition worked perfectly. Over the next nine years, I moved from project manager to vice president, then president, and finally completed the purchase of the company in 2023. I'm grateful to Mark Wilson for allowing me the opportunity to implement the philosophy of being a builder to a brand-new generation.

Tools for Your Toolbox

Building a blueprint for belief in yourself and building a philosophy to live by will help you navigate the trying times in your life and your career.

By listening to others who are detached from the situation, you gain greater perspective.

Throughout the entire story in this chapter, I constantly listened to those around me. The loyalty I had to the company and the perception of my situation did not allow me to see the true picture of my situation both mentally and physically.

I want to be clear—this was not a snap decision because of a couple of things I didn't like. Little things changed over time, and none of them were significant in themselves. When this happens to you, I challenge you to ask the questions I asked of myself.

- "Do you believe you can effect change?
- "Can you adapt your philosophy without compromising your values?"

If the changes you are making go against your philosophy or your blueprint, it may be time to build a new path to be able to implement your philosophy most effectively.

Through a lot of discussion and thought, I realized that my philosophy differed from my former company.

As the employee or the leader, you need to do a lot of soul-searching to determine what you believe before you make any decision. You must build your philosophy in your own mind to allow you to make the best decision for you and your long-term future. Ego, title, and money do not have a place in this process. Whatever you do for a living or whatever challenge you may experience, stress, deadlines, and unrealistic expectations will always be present.

You need to be a builder for yourself first. Draw up the blueprint for your values, philosophy, and culture, then face the challenge head-on. Whether you are selecting the company and the culture you want to be a part of or on the difficult path to solve a challenging issue, be true to your blueprint, and in the long run you will be successful.

The Tools

1. Build a blueprint for belief in yourself and a philosophy to live by. It will be a frame of reference when things get muddy.

2. Listen to others who are detached from the situation to gain greater perspective. Listening is the key, not acting. Remember, you are trying to gain a better perspective for things you may not have considered.

3. You need to be a builder for yourself first. Just like the masks dropping from the ceiling in a plane, put on your mask first. Only then can you be effective at helping other people.

11

BUILDING THOSE AROUND YOU

Over your life and career, you have met hundreds of leaders and managers—some who inspired you to be better and some who made you want to change jobs because you didn't want to be around them. For a large part of my career, I was the latter. It's not that I didn't want the best for the people around me or for us all to have a successful project. I was so frustrated with things not going exactly as I had planned and, well, making me look bad in front of my boss that a lot of people around me did not want to work with me. Maybe you have experienced the same type of person, or maybe you are just as frustrated as I was with the people around you. They just don't understand, right?

Since you're reading this book, I know you have a drive to learn and improve yourself. You want to know how to approach the challenges that hit you every day. You have a need to grow into a better manager and leader for those around you and for your own well-being.

The stress you are feeling comes from a gap in what you need to have done and what they can do for you. Or it could be a gap in perspective or perception of a challenge that needs to be spanned between you to move forward. You need to solve the problem. I always thought the problem was with me or the other person, but the gap is the problem, not you or the other person. I didn't believe that for a long time either. "That person is the one causing my problems; he is not performing. He is the problem."

As an example, let me tell you another story about Eddie earlier in his career. As a project administrator, Eddie was ready to be an assistant project manager, and he hit the proverbial wall in his transition to management from administration—just as I did in my first half marathon.

Eddie is an honest, hardworking, ethical person who wants to do well for himself, others, and the project. His skills as a project administrator were stellar; he could track and process information on a project with the best. It was time for him to move to an assistant project manager position to allow him to grow. He was confident coming into his new role and said, "I am ready for the challenge, boss."

I looked at him, smiled, and said, "I know you are, Eddie, and I want to give you the same advice Tim gave to me when I was in your position. Eddie," I said, "nothing is ever as good or as bad as it seems. You will get pulled through a knothole on this project, and it will be hard, but the things you will learn from the challenges and failures will take you to the next level in your career. Stay strong and stick with it."

With a quick "Got it, boss," he was off to take on the project with immense enthusiasm.

During the project, we encountered massive delays due to the pandemic and delivery of materials. We also found a bust in our bid that would eliminate most of the profit on the project, and we had a subcontractor almost go out of business. To add to the stress, it was all-hands-on-deck from the office to help and oversee everything we could. Joe and Cole, our vice president and director of construction, were trying everything they could to help the team and motivate them to keep pushing through. Joe, Cole, and I had been working together for twenty years. We had all been mentored by Tim, and I had hired them straight out of Fresno State. We all had the same builder philosophy, and I trusted everything they did. But the stress was getting to them, and it was impacting their perspective and their ability to look ahead and plan as well as hold the trades accountable for delays. This was the ultimate knothole, and Eddie was directly in the middle of it.

One day Eddie came into my office looking completely defeated. "Doug, I can't do this anymore."

I asked, "Why? Why are you feeling like that?"

"The trades aren't performing. They won't listen to me. I have done everything I can do. I'm not even sure if I want to be in construction anymore."

I sat back in my chair as I realized the gravity of the situation. I had known Eddie for years and had never seen him this defeated.

I said, "Eddie, when I asked why, you told me about the trades and what they are not doing. I want to talk about you and find out why you are feeling this way."

He said, "I'm feeling this way because no one around me will do their job!"

"Eddie, I have confidence in you, and we all have been where you are. It's hard." I reminded him about a book we read as a company called *Extreme Ownership* by Jocko Willink and Leif Babin.

I asked, "Do you remember what the main theme of the book was?"

He said, "Yeah, owning everything in your world and leadership is the solution for everything."

I said, "Right!"

He snapped, "But how can I take ownership for what they are doing wrong?"

I sat back and smiled, and he realized what he had said.

"Doug, I have tried everything I know how to do, and I'm out of ideas."

I said, "Eddie, you are out of options because you are still learning and growing in your career. You don't have all the answers, and you never will. It's having a mindset of realizing your weaknesses and building on them to make you stronger."

I asked him, "What are the three words on the back of your shirt below the collar?"

He said, "Listen Plan Build."

"Good, and what is our why?"

"To be a builder in everything we do, every day."

I said, "These are not just words; they are a process, and you must use them in that order. Right now, your team is in a panic and has skipped to the third word, *Build*. Now that you have vented, you need to connect with your team and listen to them to truly learn what is going on and what is driving them and the issues. Then solve the problem, focus on what you can do, and always find a way to move forward and improve your situation. Communicate and collaborate on a plan everyone can agree to. Then and only then can you take effective action and build the project.

"If you can build a good schedule, build consensus on your team, and finally build a system of accountability, you will finish this project successfully. This is a tough project, and you are trying to carry it all on your shoulders. Cole, Joe, and I will be right beside you, but we want you to take the lead and work through the challenges. It will pay off for you in the long run.

"Eddie, this won't happen overnight, but over time you will develop the skills to apply the philosophy of Listen Plan Build."

Looking much better, he left my office and started to implement the principles of being a builder. A couple of months later, he finished the project. He had started down the path to being a builder and a leader, but it would ultimately take a couple more projects before he had the light bulb moment as you saw in Chapter 6, but for now, let's analyze a concept Eddie was dealing with.

Tools for Your Toolbox

At first Eddie had a hard time seeing that a problem was just a thing, not a person. Ultimately, he came to realize that he had not provided a clear path for his trade contractors, he had not communicated the conditions of the market or the long lead times for materials to the owner, and he had not held his team accountable. Once he started to build knowledge, consensus, and understanding, his team and the trade contractors began to perform. Why? Because they understood where they needed to go for the betterment of the project and ultimately for the full team of all the contractors on the project.

Here's the secret: In 99% of the cases, there is a lack of understanding, confidence, skill, perspective, or knowledge causing the problem for that person. But we have a hard time separating the problem from the person. It could be as simple as they are having a bad day. It could be that they are in deeper than they thought and don't have the confidence or skill to finish the task. When that happens, the solution is for you to be a builder. Detach yourself from the situation and repeat the process.

1. **Listen** with curiosity.
2. Put a **plan** together of how to approach the situation.
3. Then **build** by taking action.

The Listen Plan Build model is a tool that allows you to detach, step back, and see a bigger picture of the situation. It helps to take the emotion out of the situation and focus on the real problem in lieu of the perceived problem. In short, it helps determine the gap (the cause) by being curious and listening. When you are building others, you are dealing with so many things that can affect the way they are feeling and how they are performing. Before you start building others, you should ask questions like:

1. "How is your day going?"
2. "You don't usually have these types of issues—what's driving the delay we are experiencing?"
3. "What resources could we bring in to make your crew more effective?"

Then, when you have a grasp on the things that are driving people during challenges, you can jump in and start building. Find a path to build. Build knowledge, build skill, build confidence, build perspective, or build understanding in everyone around you. When you do, 99% of the time the problem will melt away. Building those around you is the key component in leadership that you must implement. You can be a leader and say follow me, but people may not follow. Why? Because you have not yet built:

1. An understanding of the goal in them
2. Confidence in the team that they can accomplish the goal
3. Trust in you and themselves
4. Belief in in the cause or themselves

You as the leader need to build that bridge to span the gap, whatever it may be, by being a builder for those around you. It's as simple as that.

The concept of Listen Plan Build is a pathway to being a true builder. You, like Eddie, may struggle with solving problems. Maybe you vent your frustration instead of tackling the problem. Maybe you see others as the problem. You are the one that can change your mindset to be a builder of people, processes, and ultimately profit. But most of all, by being a builder and using the Listen Plan Build blueprint, you can immediately impact your team and be a more effective leader.

The Tools

1. A problem is just a thing, not a person. Put the problem on the table and work through it together.

2. Find a path to build. Build knowledge, build skill, build confidence, build perspective, or build understanding in everyone around you. Find alignment with your team, and you will be more effective as a leader.

3. By being a builder for those around you, you can build a bridge to span the gap, whatever it may be, for the best solution.

12

THE CHALLENGE—BUILDING FOR A CAUSE BIGGER THAN YOURSELF

You have read about building yourself and building others and how it will help you to navigate the challenges and bridge the gaps you may encounter along the way.

I have been asked by many colleagues and coworkers what keeps me going when the struggles get to be too much to bear. I tell them they need to rephrase the question. It is not about what keeps me going—it's about *why* I keep going. For me it's all about being a builder in everything I do every day. I know I will never achieve perfection in the statement; the bar is high. However, it gives me something to aspire to when challenges arise. It is a cause bigger than me.

Being a builder in everything you do will give you a mindset to approach challenges in a different way. Building others is a cause bigger than yourself. As Mahatma Gandhi says, "The best way to find yourself is to lose yourself in the services of others." Serving or building others is the essence of what Gandhi was saying. You will learn more about yourself through service to others. You will also discover and gain confidence in your "why," which will be more fulfilling than any promotion or perk you could gain at work.

To dig a little deeper, you may be thinking that you have tried to build others, but they just don't get it, or they don't acknowledge it. I submit that you may not be seeing it yet. Building is not a short-term game. It is the effect you have over time.

Fred Rogers said, "If you could only sense how important you are to the lives of those you meet; how important you can be to the people you may never even dream of. There is something you leave at every meeting with another person."[4] You touch so many lives every day. You have an impact on them in ways that you will never know. By being a builder, you are intentionally making an effort to build on the successes and failures of yourself and those around you. That is truly a cause bigger than yourself.

The Red Jeep

If you are in the process of looking for or discovering a new path, I can tell you that you won't find it unless you are looking for it. To emphasize that point, in 2019, my wife announced that she wanted to get a new car. She loved her Juke but wanted something a little more fun and rugged. She said she wanted a new Jeep Wrangler, and it had to be red with a manual transmission.

I said, "A Jeep? I don't see any Jeeps on the road anymore, and I've heard they have a lot of problems."

She said, "I see them all the time; they are everywhere. I researched the Wrangler, and it has a great quality record."

The conversation went back and forth for a while, and we decided to go test drive a Jeep over the weekend.

The next day on my way to work (about a 30-minute drive), to my astonishment, it seemed like every other car I saw was a JEEP! They were everywhere, and a lot of them were RED! It was incredible!

---

4   Fred Rogers, *The World According to Mister Rogers: Important Things to Remember* (New York: Hachette Books, 2003).

I called Jodi. She picked up the phone, and the first thing I said was "I'm sorry."

She said, "Sorry for what?"

I said, "Hun, I just saw 83 RED JEEPS ON THE WAY TO WORK!"

We both broke out laughing.

The moral of the story is: If you're not looking for it, you will never see it.

If you are thinking about being a builder, you will see so many opportunities and examples all around you every day. You will see the builders, and you will see the opportunities to build.

Discovering My Why

If you remember, I was struggling at work and at home because I was driven by promotions, success, and thinking too much about myself. I recognized that I was looking for something, but I just couldn't find it. Well, sometimes answers come in the least expected areas.

In late 2008, we finished a small portable classroom project that was to be used for a kindergarten classroom in a small rural school district. It was simple, nothing complex, just a humble portable classroom building. For our project manager, this was his first project to lead on his own. Just a few days before school started, the school district wanted to bring the community and the students who would be using the classroom together to do a ribbon cutting for the project.

I have done hundreds of ribbon cuttings over the course of my career, and they never cease to amaze me. Watching the smiles on the faces of the students, the doctors and nurses, and the parishioners and pastors always brought me joy and a sense of accomplishment. I was usually the one saying a few words about the construction team and thanking the designers and the owner for a great project. This time, I decided to take a step back and have the new project manager give the ribbon-cutting speech. He was excited but also nervous and anxious. He worked on the speech for a few days prior and ran it by me the day before the event. He wrote a great speech, and I told him to enjoy the moment and soak in the people who were there to enjoy what he had built.

On the day of the ribbon cutting, our project manager walked to the podium and unfolded his speech. As he looked over the crowd, his eyes moved down to the front row where 17 future kindergarten students sat in the red-and-blue T-shirts representing the school. He looked down at his speech, then looked up at the kids again.

He said, "Well, I had a speech prepared for all of you today, but I think I am just going to say a few words to these smiling faces right here down front." With that, he folded his speech, set it down, and spoke directly to the kids.

He enthusiastically said, "Hi, guys! I got to meet your teacher, and she is amazing. She has some fun things planned for you this year. Are you excited?"

All the kids yelled, "Yeah!"

By this time, our project manager had a huge smile on his face. All his nerves were gone, and he was in the moment just talking to the kids.

He continued, "I'm really happy we got to build this new classroom for you. You are going to meet so many new friends and learn so many cool things this year, and someday you are going to grow up and be anything you want to be. Thank you for letting me be here."

He walked from the podium and went down to the front row and shook the hand of every single student. The crowd erupted, and the kids cheered.

On the way back to the office, I asked him why he decided to change his speech.

He said, "Doug, after all the problems we had on the project, all the challenges we overcame, standing in front of those kids, it all went away. I finally understand what you mean. We build for the kids. It's not about the structure. It's all about what they get to learn and the friendships they will make because of the building we built."

At that moment, I made a discovery in my own mind and philosophy. It wasn't that I was proud of the building we built; it was what came out of the building that hit me. I had been involved with nearly 100 projects at that point in my career, but I had never looked at it from that perspective. I realized that the students got to build friendships and knowledge because of the new classroom we built, and the teacher was the one that became their builder.

Building for People You May Never Meet

Building for people you may never meet may seem like an impossible task, but you already do it every day. As a part of a team, you may pass on knowledge that the team can use to solve a problem in the future when you are not there. As a parent, you have raised your kids to leave your house and succeed on their own. But they take with them all the family dinners and discussions, the morals and philosophy, all of which will help them make better decisions and give them the confidence that they can achieve anything they strive for. Your purpose as a builder is not created with the buildings or things you build. It is rooted with your teammates, your family, and the people who will use the building, product, or information you've provided.

While building a building and then being able to stand back and see the result of my work is rewarding, there is a larger cause that has come to mean much more. For me, it's about the people who will use the building after construction is completed—many of whom I will never meet. The people using the building, in my mind, are the ultimate builders. They have an amazing impact on our communities, our country, and our world.

To give you an example in construction, building schools will allow teachers to **BUILD knowledge in their students**, building medical facilities will allow doctors to **BUILD health for the community**, and building churches will allow pastors to **BUILD faith in their parishioners**.

If you are not in the construction world, you can still be a builder in your own field and in your community. Insurance carriers build stability; accountants build financial security; bus drivers build connections for their community; sanitation workers build clean cities. Everyone can be a builder for a cause bigger than themselves.

On an individual basis, building knowledge in those around you will allow them to build better solutions in the future. Building trust with colleagues and clients will build better relationships in the long run. Building confidence in your team will allow them to step forward into challenges when they are uncertain.

The Challenge

Be a builder in everything you do. Being a builder is a high standard that will be difficult to achieve in the short term and so rewarding in the long term. You must have a growth mindset for yourself and those around you.

I believe that everyone can be a builder, no matter what job they do or what position they hold. Every person brings different qualities as well as the ability to learn and grow. We can't possibly do it individually, but together we can.

Your aim should be to walk beside the next generation of builders and inspire them to carry on the philosophy of "being a builder." Seek out those future builders and invest the time and energy to mentor them. Challenge them to be better and instill in them the mindset and culture of being a builder. Embrace challenges as small gaps you can close by building a bridge. Use Listen Plan Build and the four mindsets as tools to build the bridges. Remember, you will have an impact on the people you meet every day whether you know it or not.

Remember, too, that all great leaders are builders. So, when you are facing a gap, get stuck, frustrated, or find yourself in a challenge that seems insurmountable, take a breath and ask yourself, "What do I need to build?" The answer will put you on a path to be an amazing leader.

I challenge you to be a builder in everything you do everyday.

REVIEW INQUIRY

Hey, builders, it's Doug Reitz here.

I hope you've enjoyed the book, finding it both useful and fun. I have a favor to ask you.

Would you consider giving it a rating wherever you bought the book? Online bookstores are more likely to promote a book when they feel good about its content, and reader reviews are a great barometer for a book's quality.

So please go to the website where you bought the book, search for my name and the book title, and leave a review. If possible, perhaps consider adding a picture of you holding the book. That increases the likelihood your review will be accepted!

Many thanks in advance,

Doug Reitz

WILL YOU SHARE THE LOVE?

Get this book for a friend, associate, or family member!

If you have found this book valuable and know others who would find it useful, consider buying them a copy as a gift. Special bulk discounts are available if you would like your whole team or organization to benefit from reading this. Just contact build@dougreitz.blog or go to dougreitz.blog.

WOULD YOU LIKE DOUG REITZ TO SPEAK TO YOUR ORGANIZATION?

Book Doug Now!

Doug Reitz accepts a limited number of speaking/coaching/training engagements each year. To learn how you can bring his message to your organization, email build@dougreitz.blog or visit dougreitz.blog.

OTHER BOOKS BY DOUG REITZ

Co-author of the #1 Best Seller
When Work Works: Cutting-Edge Solutions for the Contemporary Workplace